STO

FRIENDS
OF ACPL

W9-DFF-745

12-15-60

The Literary Riddle Before 1600

THE
LITERARY RIDDLE
BEFORE 1600

Archer Taylor

UNIVERSITY OF CALIFORNIA PRESS
Berkeley and Los Angeles
1948

University of California Press
Berkeley and Los Angeles
California

❖

Cambridge University Press
London, England

COPYRIGHT, 1948, BY
THE REGENTS OF THE UNIVERSITY OF CALIFORNIA

PRINTED IN THE UNITED STATES OF AMERICA
BY THE UNIVERSITY OF CALIFORNIA PRESS

PREFACE

1147785

T HE FOLLOWING ACCOUNT *of a minor literary genre extends to the time when it was recognized as worthy of special anthologies and treatises on its history and technique; in other words, to about 1600. I hope to examine the subsequent development of the art at a later time. Since Michele De Filippis has studied separately the efflorescence of riddling in Italy, I have limited my Italian references to the quotation of parallels generously supplied by him and have not sought to give a systematic treatment of them. Literary historians have usually given little or no attention to the texts examined here, and furthermore, many of them are difficult of access. This essay has therefore the defects that naturally attach to a first survey of an untilled field.*

A.T.

CONTENTS

Chapter I

THE POPULAR AND THE LITERARY RIDDLE

IN THE STUDY of folklore it is desirable to separate popular or folk materials and literary, learned, or artistic materials. Literary or learned men have often imitated or adapted the various kinds of folklore. Their imitations are rarely intended to deceive and can usually be recognized without difficulty. The popular ballad may have inspired Dante Gabriel Rossetti to write *Sister Helen*. Heinrich Heine was writing in the popular vein when he composed *Die Lorelei*. Oriental tales, many of them ultimately of folk origin, flooded Europe in the eighteenth century and gave rise to literary tales conceived in the popular manner.

Like the ballad and the tale, the riddle has popular and literary forms. A popular or folk riddle draws attention to the similarity between two wholly unrelated objects by a very simple rhetorical device.[1] The speaker relates the adventure of a certain Humpty

---

[1] In the following study I shall use the term "riddle" in the meaning which is defined here. Many varieties of puzzling questions are loosely called riddles. Arithmetical problems, conundrums, questions requiring for the answer a shrewd wit, questions demanding a knowledge of the Bible, and many other kinds of puzzles are sometimes called riddles, but I shall not use the term in so broad a sense. These puzzles also appear in popular and literary versions.

Dumpty who sits on a wall and falls from it. He then suddenly tells us that an egg is intended. He has confused us by the simple device of speaking first in general terms which can be taken in two ways, and then in specific terms which can be taken in only one way. A vague general description contrasts sharply with a specific description that follows it. "Humpty Dumpty sat on a wall" and "Humpty Dumpty had a great fall" are simple statements apparently referring to a man. The conclusion,

> All the king's horses and all the king's men
> Can't put Humpty Dumpty together again,

does not fit a man. After a fall a man would probably recover and at least would not need to be put together. The contradiction warns us that Humpty Dumpty is no ordinary man and leads us to seek the explanation found in the answer: egg. In other words, a folk riddle contrasts a vague description with one that is understood literally. Since it consists of two brief descriptions, it is itself quite brief.

The literary riddle also describes something in terms of objects entirely different from the answer. A typical illustration is the Renaissance English butterfly riddle:

> First I was small, and round like a pearl;
> Then long and slender, as brave as an earl;
> Since, like an hermit, I lived in a cell,
> And now, like a rogue, in the wide world I dwell.[2]

---

[2] *The Riddles of Heraclitus and Democritus* (1598), no. 27, reprinted in Brandl, p. 38. I have modernized the spelling.

Similar comparisons might be found in folk riddles. The confusing notion of a person who is both small and round as well as long and slender occurs in the Renaissance English riddle for a ball of thread:"What is that: round as a ball, longer than Paul's steeple, weather-cocke, and all?"[3] Here the descriptive details offer a contrast, but the personification of the ball is only vaguely suggested. The butterfly riddle also sets living like a hermit over against wandering like a rogue. A folk riddle might conceivably use such a contrast. The fact that the speaker describes himself by these details is hardly enough to unify the conception. The listener is overwhelmed by unrelated details. Such an *embarras de richesses* is characteristic of the literary riddle.

The literary riddle ordinarily contains a long series of assertions and contradictions and is often put in the form of a speech made by the object that is being described. In order to accumulate details enough to permit the listener to guess the answer, the riddler often sacrifices the unity of his conception. The first assertion and its denial are almost certain to conflict with the next pair. Yet the author goes on and on, while his conception becomes more and more incoherent. In the butterfly riddle, he has been shrewd enough to tie the details together in a biography, but the unity thus gained is somewhat superficial. Literary riddles do not often contradict a vague general description with specific details.

---

[3] Taylor, *English Riddles from Oral Tradition* (in press), no. 1342.

The authors of literary riddles often choose themes which are never employed by folk riddlers. Abstract subjects, for example, are rarely used by folk riddlers. The few riddles in folk tradition that have abstract answers are probably derived from learned sources. Of some we may, however, be in doubt. The German riddle for a riddle has something of the folk flavor:

> Kennst du mich,
> So freut es dich;
> Kennst du mich nicht,
> So suche mich
> Nur emsiglich:
> Du findest mich
> Ganz sicherlich.[4]

The Swedes have a shorter version to much the same effect, in which a riddle is conceived as a thing and not a person: "When one does not know what it is, then it is something; but when one knows what it is, then it is nothing."[5] Riddles of this sort may be of folk origin or may have acquired some characteristics of folk riddles. If we set them beside a sonnet by Catone l'Uticense,[6] we see clearly the difference between the folk riddle and the art riddle. Catone writes:

> Di chiaro Genitor oscuro Figlio,
>> Ma quanto oscuro più tanto più bello:
>> Sconosciuto men vò; ma mai son quello,
>> Che a l'aspetto rassembro, e che somiglio.

---

[4] Simrock, *Das deutsche Rätselbuch,* 3d ed. (Basel, n.d.), p. 86. Quoted by Pitrè, *Indovinelli, dubbi, scioglilingua del popolo siciliano* (Turin and Palermo, Clausen, 1897), p. xx.

[5] Sandén, "Norra Vadsbo," p. 36, no. 197.

[6] This is a pseudonym for Francesco Maurello or Leone Santucci.

Varie sembianze, e strane forme piglio,
Facendomi così Proteo novello.
Quei, che già sa chi son, come m'appello,
Vien per saper chi son meco a consiglio.

Senza nulla levar di quanto tegno
Intorno per vestir, mi può scoprire
Tutto da capo a piè chi ha qualche ingegno.

Non ve l'abbiate a mal; io vi so dire,
Che 'l mio gusto maggior, vanto il più degno,
È il vedervi per me starvi a impazzire.[7]

A still better definition of a riddle is given by Cervantes:

Es muy escura, y es clara;
Tiene mil contrariedades;
Encubrenos las verdades,
Y al cabo nos las declara.
Nasce a vezes de donayre,
otras, de altas fantasias,
y suele engendrar porfias,
aunque trate cosas de ayre.

Sabe su nombre qualquiera,
hasta los niños pequeños;
son muchas, y tienen dueños
de diferente manera.
No ay vieja que no se abrace
con una destas señoras;
son de gusto algunas horas:
qual cansa, qual satisfaze.

---

[7] *Enimmi* di Catone l'Uticense Lucchese (Genoa, Franchelli, 1761), p. 1,
no. 1.

> Sabios ay que se desuelan
> por sacarles los sentidos,
> y algunos quedan corridos
> quanto mas sobre ello velan.
> Qual es nescia, qual curiosa,
> qual facil, qual intricada,
> pero sea o no sea nada,
> dezidme que es cosa y cosa.[8]

In a sense, the last line gives away the answer, for
cosa y cosa (thing and thing) means also riddle. Cervantes makes the characteristic error of the learned
riddler in failing to describe, without admitting ex-
traneous matter, an object which is not the intended
answer.

This fault does not appear in a sonnet that Galileo
Galilei wrote on reading the first part of Antonio
Malatesti's riddles:

> Mostro son'io più strano e più deforme
>   che l'Arpia, la Sirena o la Chimera;
>   nè in terra, in aria, in acqua è alcuna fiera,
>   ch'abbia di membra così varie forme.
> Parte a parte non ò, che sia conforme:
>   più che s'una sia bianca, e l'altra nera;
>   spesso di Cacciator dietro ò una schiera,
>   che de' miei piè van rintracciando l'orme.
> Nelle tenebre oscure è il mio soggiorno,
>   che se dall'ombre al chiaro lume passo,
>   tosto l'alma da me sen fugge, come

---

[8] *La Galatea*, ed. Schevill and Bonilla y San Martín (Madrid, 1914),
Book VI, pp. 259–260.

> Sen fugge il sonno all'apparir del giorno,
>   e le mie membra disunite lasso,
>   e l'esser perdo con la vita, e 'l nome.[9]

Here Galileo has adopted the technique of the folk riddle by comparing the answer to something quite different from it. He leads the hearer astray by pointing out the resemblances, and he holds throughout to a single theme. He does not, however, sharply contrast a vague general description and a specific detail. His choice of a comparison to a monster that is rendered powerless by knowing its name—a comparison which was suggested by the story of the Sphinx—smells of the lamp.

Many literary riddles make obscene suggestions.[10] They usually develop the theme with an evident delight in seeing how far it can be carried and yet leave an opportunity to defeat the hearer with an innocent answer. Although folk riddles also employ the same device, they guide the hearer by a single statement.

Not a few literary riddles give evidence of being a deliberate artistic elaboration of the folk theme. This seems true of the Scotch

> Robbers came to our house
>   And we were all in;
> The house leaped out at the windows
>   And we were all ta'n.[11]

---

[9] Antonio Malatesti, *La Sfinge e la Tina* (ed. Allodoli, 1913), p. 18.

[10] For a detailed discussion of this topic see Michele De Filippis, *The Literary Riddle in Italy to the End of the Sixteenth Century* (Univ. Calif. Publ. Mod. Philol., Vol. XXXIV, No. 1, 1948), pp. 12–17, 38–40, 41, 43, 50, 55, 65–69, 89, 91, 93–95.

[11] Chambers, *Popular Rhymes of Scotland* (1870), p. 12.

A French version from Brittany will adequately illustrate the folk conception: "Les voleurs ont pris moi et ma maison; ma maison sort par les croisées, et moi seule je reste en prison. Un poisson pris au carrelet."[12] In the version of Larivey, who substituted it for Straparola's Unicorn (*Notti*, XIII, 1), this riddle assumes a wholly literary form and becomes:

J'estois en ma maison vivant paisiblement,
Loin des mutins débats d'une guerre intestine,
Quand je fus assailly d'une trope mutine,
Qui me tint assiégé assez estroictement.

Hardy, je resistay dès le commencement
A ses plus durs assaux, et d'une ruse fine,
Me pensant garantir d'une proche ruine,
Or deçà, or delà, m'eschappay finement.

Toutesfois, à la fin je ne peu si bien faire
Que ne tombasse és mains de ce fier adversaire,
Qui, si tost qu'il m'eut prins, cruel, me mit à mort.

Et ce malheur n'advint par ma maison, qui dextre
Les sentant approcher, saulta par la fenestre,
Et s'enfuit, me laissans sans aide et sans support.[13]

The main enigmatic quality of this riddle—the seeming impossibility of discovering a house (water) which leaps out of its windows (meshes of a net)—has been

---

[12] Sébillot, "Devinettes," p. 100, no. 22. For the discussion of many parallels of this popular riddle see Gaston Paris in Rolland, pp. ix–x; Rodríguez Marín, p. 337; Pitrè, *Indovinelli*, pp. lxxi–lxxvii; Tupper, *The Riddles of the Exeter Book*, p. 225, no. 85, and *Modern Language Notes*, XVIII (1903), 3, 5; Taylor, *English Riddles*, no. 906.

[13] *Les Facétieuses Nuits de Straparole*, traduit par Jean Louveau et Pierre de Larivey (Paris, Jannet, 1857), Vol. II, p. 345.

retained in both the popular and the literary versions, but the progress made in the elaboration of the same theme is remarkable.

The counterparts to folk themes that have been raised to the level of art are the literary riddles that have degenerated in the process of oral transmission.

Frederick Tupper has admirably stated the distinction between the Kunsträtsel and the Volksrätsel. He writes:

This distinction is not always easy to recognize, on account of the close connection between the two types. . . . The literary riddle may consist largely or entirely of popular elements, may be (and often is) an elaborated version of an original current in the mouth of the folk; conversely, the popular riddle is often found in germ or in full development in some product of the study, and our task is to trace its transmission from scholar to peasant. Through a more complicated sequence, a genuine folk riddle may be adapted in an artistic version which in a later day or in another land becomes again common property; or, by a natural corollary, a literary riddle, having passed into the stock of countryside tradition, may fail of its popular life and survive only in some pedantic reworking that knows nothing of the earlier art form. Even after the thorough examination of the style and the careful investigation of the history of each riddle so urgently recommended by Petsch and hitherto so much neglected, we cannot be sure that this apparently popular product is not an adaptation of some classical original, or that this enigma smelling so strongly of the lamp is not a reshaping of some puzzle of peasants.... [Petsch] notes that the typical Volksrätsel is confined to a

scanty framework, a hurried statement of the germ ele-
ment, naïve description, a sudden check in our progress to
the goal of the solution, and finally a word of summary. In
literary enigmas . . . all these divisions may and do appear,
but each of them is patiently elaborated with a conscious
delight in workmanship and rhythm, with a regard for
detail that overlooks no aspect of the theme, however
trivial—in a word, with a poetic subordination of the end
in view to the finish of the several parts.[14]

[14] Preface to *Exeter Book*, pp. xvi–xvii.

Chapter II

THE HISTORY OF THE
LITERARY RIDDLE

ITERARY RIDDLES have been written at many times and in many places. We can often trace a continuous tradition from a Sanskrit ritual more than two thousand years old to a college dean writing in his study today. The survival of themes through such vicissitudes is an interesting and instructive example of the preservation of intellectual matters. Oriental riddlers have freely borrowed themes from one another, particularly the themes of the world or the year, which are often identified with that of the sun. The great popularity of certain authors, of whom Al-Harîrî, the Arabic riddlemaster of Bassorah, is a notable example, and of certain stories in which, as in the legend of Aḥiḳar, belonging to the first Christian centuries, riddles are embedded, justifies us in inferring the existence of an active literary tradition. The records are, however, incomplete and often difficult of access. The tracing of influences demands a critical acquaintance with the stylistic peculiarities of these languages and literatures. A history of Oriental riddling is something to be desired, both for itself and for the light it will throw on developments in the West, but it is likely to remain an unfulfilled wish.

In Greece and Constantinople the situation is somewhat clearer: the records are more abundant and the influence of one writer on another is often perceived. Although no one has written an account of medieval Greek riddling, several have proposed undertaking the task.

The development of Latin riddling is traceable primarily to Symphosius, an author (according to the best recent opinions) of the fifth century A.D. He was the model of Anglo-Latin enigmatographs in the seventh and eighth centuries and, through them, of both an Old English riddlemaster and later writers of the continent of Europe. He maintained his sovereign place down to the time of the Renaissance, and even later, as the master of the enigmatic art. In the following pages we shall review hastily literary riddling to the end of the sixteenth century.[1]

Since the sharp separation of literature and folklore has come about only slowly, we often find little difference between the riddles of art and the riddles of the folk as we go backward in time. The oldest riddles often present difficult and indeed insoluble problems in differentiating the shares of art and of the folk. The oldest recorded riddles are Babylonian school texts

---

[1] There has been no previous history of the literary riddle, and the present attempt has therefore all the faults of a first sketch. The general remarks of Frederick Tupper in the preface to *The Riddles of the Exeter Book* (Boston, 1910) are excellent but all too brief. He had no occasion to go far beyond Symphosius and his imitators. J. B. Friedreich's *Geschichte des Räthsels* (Dresden, 1860), although often condemned as the work of a dilettante, is still the best account of the literary riddle. See also the Introduction to Pitrè, *Indovinelli*.

which show no literary polish.[2] Yet the use of these texts in a schoolbook is, in a sense, a recognition of them as a literary form. Since the answers are lacking, we are forced to supply them by conjecture. A description such as "My knees hasten, my feet do not rest, a shepherd without pity drives me to pasture" might suggest a river that runs without ceasing and a rower who moves the oars back and forth. "You went and took the enemy's property; the enemy came and took your property" might be a shuttle passing to and fro. "Who becomes pregnant without conceiving, who becomes fat without eating?" is probably a rain cloud. A reference to a chest of silver and a casket of gold offers difficulties to the translator, but is obviously an egg. It is clear that we have here riddles from oral tradition that a teacher has put into a schoolbook.

Some very old Sanskrit riddles that are in part literary and in part popular in origin have been dressed up for use in ritual.[3] The oldest of them are in the Rigveda, which is usually ascribed to a time not far from the beginning of the first millennium B.C. They occur, however, in a hymn in the first book, which is usually regarded as somewhat later in date than the

---

[2] M. Jaeger, "Assyrische Räthsel und Sprichwörter," *Beiträge zur Assyriologie*, II (1894), 274–305. A Sumerian original accompanying the Assyrian text shows that the collection was intended for use as a schoolbook.

[3] See [Martin] Haug, "Vedische Räthselfragen und Räthselsprüche," *Sitzungsberichte d. k. Akad. d. Wissenschaften, philosophisch-philologische Classe* (Munich), II, No. 3 (1875); Moritz Winternitz, *A History of Indian Literature*, Index.

core of the collection. A slightly different and somewhat shorter version containing forty-seven riddles
is found in the Atharvaveda.⁴ It is supposed that the
latter version is the original form of the hymn. Parallels to the five additional riddles of the version in the
first book of the Rigveda are found elsewhere in Vedic
texts. Except for one verse, which contains three
catechetical questions, these riddles are of the folk
type. Except for these three questions, the answers to
the riddles are lacking and have been the occasion of
much speculation, even in ancient times. A typical
riddle is: "The one who made him does not know him.
He escapes from the one who has seen him. Enveloped
in his mother's womb, he is subject to annihilation,
while he has many descendants."⁵ Lightning, which
is not very satisfactory, is only one of the many
answers that have been proposed. Perhaps wind is
better, as suggested by Karl F. Geldner.⁶ Somewhat
more of a literary atmosphere is apparent in: "Breath-
ing, it lies there and is nevertheless quick in its gait,
moving and yet fixed in the rivers. The soul of the
dead man goes about as it likes. The immortal one has
the same origin as the mortal one."⁷ Some think that

---

⁴ Rigveda, I, 164, 34–35; Atharvaveda, 9, 9–10. See also the Bṛhadde-
vata, 4, 31–43. This ancient commentary has been edited by A. A. Mac-
donell (Harvard Oriental Series, Vols. V, VI, Cambridge, 1904). Like the
much later Sāyna, this contains some answers to the riddles. See also selections in Alfred Hillebrandt, *Lieder des Ṛgveda* (Göttingen, 1913), pp.
103–105.

⁵ Rigveda, I, 164, 32. Haug suggests the answer: lightning.

⁶ *Der Rigveda* (Göttingen, 1928), I, 211.

⁷ Rigveda, I, 164, 30. See also R. Roth, "Zwei Sprüche über Leib und
Seele," *Zeitschrift der Deutschen morgenländischen Gesellschaft,* XLVI
(1892), 759.

the answer is body and soul; others suggest that it is
Agni. Much to the same effect is: "It moves freely
backwards and forwards, although imprisoned. The
immortal one has the same origin as the mortal one.
In the course of time the two separate, going in this
and that direction. If we see one of them, we do not
see the other."[8] The style reminds us of the popular
riddle, but the themes, so far as we can perceive them,
are literary rather than popular.

The characteristic themes of the riddles in the Rigveda are cosmological. Some have seen the sun in "I
saw a restless shepherd traveling back and forth on
his paths. He garbs himself in that which goes in the
same and in an opposite direction. He goes hither and
thither among creatures."[9] Such conceptions of the
sun or moon are not unusual in folk riddling. The
reference to herds of creatures suggests the stars and
leads one to think of the stars rather than the moon
as the answer. Since, however, Geldner, a recent and
highly esteemed translator, gives us now the answer,
breath, we see the difficulties that students of these
Vedic riddles must face. A simple example of the
many Vedic riddles for the year is: "The wheel of
nature with twelve spokes turns around the heavens
without ever going to ruin. On it stand, O Agni, sons
in pairs to the number of seven hundred and twenty."[10]

---

[8] Rigveda, I, 164, 38. See Roth, p. 760. Geldner suggests that the answer
is inhaling and exhaling.

[9] Rigveda, I, 164, 31. See also Geldner's translation.

[10] Rigveda, I, 164, 11. For several literary riddles dealing with the year
see pp. 39, 68, 71, 102–103, 108, below, and De Filippis, pp. 14, 59–60, 77.

In the Viśve devāḥ (Rigveda, VIII, 29)[11] ten gods are described in enigmatic stanzas of this sort:

> One is brown, varied in form, beautiful, young.
> He adorns himself with golden ornament.—Soma.

and

> One bears a bolt placed in his hand:
> With it he slays his foes.—Indra.

In an interchange of questions and answers the Mahābharata[12] recites an outline of Indian ethics. A typical stanza is:

> Who is the friend of the traveler? Who is the friend of him who remains at home? Who is the friend of the sick? Who is the friend of the dying?

> A caravan is the friend of the traveler. The wife is the friend of him who remains at home. The doctor is the friend of the sick. Charity is the friend of the dying.

The highly sophisticated quality of many Sanskrit riddles can perhaps be adequately illustrated by one rather simple example of an invention like a charade: "Who moves in the air? Who makes a noise on seeing a thief? Who is the enemy of lotuses? Who is the climax of fury?"[13] The answers to the first three questions, when combined in the manner of a charade, yield the answer to the fourth question. The first answer is bird (*vi*), the second dog (*çva*), the third sun

---

[11] A. A. Macdonnell, *A Vedic Reader for Students* (Oxford, 1917), pp. 147–152.

[12] III, 313, 65 f. See Moritz Winternitz, *A History of Indian Literature* (Calcutta, 1927), I, 352–353.

[13] A. Führer, "Sanskrit-Räthsel," *Zeitschrift der Deutschen morgenländischen Gesellschaft*, XXXIX (1885), 99–100.

(*mitra*), and the whole is Viçvamitra, Rama's first teacher and counselor and a man noted for his outbursts of rage.

Although our information about Chinese riddling is scanty, it includes references to several kinds of puzzling problems and to customs implying a familiarity with art riddles.[14] In the first decade of the twelfth century, schools of riddlers flourished in the bazaars of Pien-liang (now K'ai-fêng-fu), which was then the capital of China. A century later, we hear of studios at Hangchow, where riddles were written and discussed. At the lantern festival, riddles were set for all participants to guess. Unfortunately, texts of medieval Chinese riddles are not available. Many Chinese riddles call for a knowledge of Chinese writing and consequently are almost impossible to translate.

Although Ḥâjjî Khalîfa's fourteenth-century bibliography is almost certainly the first work of the kind to give attention to riddles as a genre, any account of the art as practiced by Arabic writers must be superficial until a competent Arabist has studied it. Many of the pertinent texts are, to be sure, in print, but neither Ḥâjjî Khalîfa's citations nor those of later authorities identify the exact passages, and a search for them, at least for a non-Arabist, is something like looking for a needle in a haystack. Much also lies buried in manuscripts, and these must be examined,

---

[14] See Richard C. Rudolph, "Notes on the Riddle in China," *California Folklore Quarterly*, I (1942), 65–82.

for the descriptions in catalogues are very summary. A satisfactory account of Arabic riddling is therefore a desideratum, and the following remarks can only suggest the richness of the field.

Ḥâjjî Khalîfa begins[15] with a very good definition of a riddle and adds an interesting remark about its use: "Utilitas tam aenigmatum quam logogriphorum eo constat, quod mens iis confirmatur et acuitur." As illustrations, he quotes two riddles by anonymous authors, one for a pen:

Quis est servus ille caput demittens et se humilians, attenuatus, lacrimas fundans,
Assidue temporibus statutis quinioni affixus, unice creatoris servitio deditus?

and another for a book:

Judex judicum, qui jus dicit tacitus; juste judicat, arcanum suum non manifestat, et tamen loquitur.
Judicat linguâ, quae non inclinat, et si ad unum adversariorum inclinat, hic justus declaratur.[16]

He then cites half a dozen writers who flourished between the fourteenth and sixteenth centuries of the Christian Era. They are far from representing fully the abundance of Arabic riddling, but it is worth noting how far specialization in the art had gone. Two of them wrote only legal riddles, a variety to which Al-Ḥarîrî devoted his fifteenth and thirty-second assemblies.

---

[15] Gustav Flügel (ed. and tr.), *Lexicon bibliographicum et encyclopaedicum a ... Haji Khalfa* (Leipzig, 1835), I, 402–404. See also IV, 376.
[16] *Ibid.*

A much more adequate bibliography of Arabic riddling will be found in René Basset's review of Giacobetti's Algerian Arabic folk riddles.[17] In his preface, Giacobetti had mentioned the eleven writers of riddles cited in the *Majânî l'Adab*, to which I shall refer later. Basset names a score of others and speaks somewhat sharply about Giacobetti's ignorance of the subject. Inasmuch as Basset gives no precise references to the authors whom he names, his list is both a challenge and an annoyance. Only two of these authors have been translated: Al-Ḥarîrî and Al-Abshîhî.

The passages intended by Basset in Al-Abshîhî's Al-Mostaṭraf, an encyclopedic collection of *loci communes* compiled in the last years of the fourteenth century, are the seventh chapter, on clarity in language, and the seventy-second, on poetry.[18] The first of these includes two lists of shrewd questions concerned with religious themes and is not pertinent to our present interests. The seventy-second chapter contains two sections on riddles. The first of these includes forty-three examples, chiefly simple versifications of folk themes. A riddle for a clog or shoe is typical:

It is a nag whose rider goes on foot. It bears its rider and its rider bears it. One leaves it at the door all muddy. It never eats nor drinks.[19]

---

[17] *Revue des traditions populaires*, XXXII (1917), 186–190.
[18] Translated by G. Rat (Paris, 1899). See esp. Vol. I, pp. 149–153, and Vol. II, pp. 545–553, 575–576.
[19] II, 545.

Among the subjects of these riddles are an inkwell, a reed pen, a book, a flute, a bracelet, the beard, a banana, a hydraulic wheel, a dress, fire, a pestle, a razor, and the eye. There are some rather fully developed literary examples: one is ascribed to a known author and others play with the name of Sultan Ḥasan or versify a charade on the name of Samarkand. A long millstone riddle contains folk themes but has passed through a poet's hands:

It always hastens on its journey, one sees it continually going forwards, and it never wearies.

During its course it never stops eating for a moment, it eats day and night, but it never drinks.

Notwithstanding its continual journeying, it never exceeds the range of five cubits, not by even one-third of one-eighth of a cubit or anything approaching that much.[19]

The four texts included in the seventy-second chapter in a second section on riddles are noteworthy. Their subjects are a lamp, the eye, a cake, and a sieve. I quote the first and the last. The lamp riddle is as follows:

What is that sea which is not of water, which increases and diminishes during the night, and in which one can neither leap nor drown;

Which contains something in the shape of a serpent, a serpent having no hole to which to retreat and having a mouth in which, O my friend, there is a thing

That one sees—there is no mistake about it—whether

---

[19] II, 545. It is printed as the riddle of an anonymous author in the *Majânî l'Adab*, III, no. 268.

one is near or far, that hides itself daily in very truth to reappear anew,

That vanishes during the day, but spreads on human faces the light of dawn as soon as night looks upon it,

That watches like a lover whom love compels and kills on hills and at the bottom of valleys?[20]

The sieve riddle, which is even more complicated, begins with the suggestion of an abnormal creature and veers into the description of a thing:

What then, is that object, O Sâ'd, that is all eyes and yet cannot distinguish profound darkness and dazzling light,

[That object] which is provided with a wooden border enclosing all the affair and which, although it is itself lifeless, nevertheless brings life to all the things necessary to existence,

[That object] which no one can dispense with in the house for a single day and which no person can take the place of, even when he wears himself out with exertions,

[That object] the use of which requires an abundance of skillfully combined motions, that overwhelms you night and morning with clouds of dust,

And [that object] which one needs always, in perpetuity, because of its frequent utility and the constant services that it renders?[21]

I shall confine my further remarks on Arabic riddling to the texts found in the *Majânî l'Adab*, a modern anthology of Arabic literature of all periods, and to Al-Ḥarîrî, the most important of Arabic riddle-

[20] II, 575.
[21] II, 576.

masters. Even this scanty selection from a very rich enigmatic literature shows that the practice of the art began early and ranged far. The earliest riddler in the *Majânî l'Adab* seems to be Ibn Sukkara al-Hâshimî (d. 995) of Bagdad. Among the fifty thousand verses that he wrote is a riddle on Ibn Berghûth (son of the flea), a friend's name: "He has put me to the test, but I cannot tell his name; all go, asking his friendship. My friend has hindered me in sleeping. If I succeed in closing my eyes, his father awakens me."[22] Although folk riddles about fleas are numerous enough, this is clearly a literary rather than a popular conceit. Between the tenth and twelfth centuries the writing of Arabic riddles flourished, and I shall reserve Al-Ḥarîrî, the most famous and influential writer of them, for special consideration. Abû Zakariya ibn Salâma al-Haṣkafî (1069–1157), who studied at Bagdad, wrote a riddle about a litter for the dead.[23] The text contains the abundance of contradictions characteristic of literary riddling. It is as follows:

> Do you know of a thing under the sky [of such a
>   sort] that when it passes
> People cry loudly as it goes by?
> You will find it ridden and riding,
> And every prince who mounts it is a prisoner.
> It incites to virtue, and its nearness is hated.
> It is a warner, and man runs away from it.

---

[22] *Majânî l'Adab*, II, no. 358. For these translations I am indebted to Mrs. Nicoletta Rosenthal-Misch.

[23] *Majânî l'Adab*, III, no. 266.

> It desires to visit, yet it is not asked to come;
> But it will come visiting, however uninvited.

The polymath Muḥammad ibn al-Khashshâb (1100–1172) of Bagdad described a book with similar contradictions:

> Though of many faces, it is no revealer of secrets;
> The two-faced one will show up the secret.
> The secrets of its face will confide to you the secrets,
> And you will hear it with the eye as long as you are
>   looking.[24]

Such toying with the word "secret" is characteristic of literary riddling, and the paradox of hearing with the eye mentioned in the last line is probably too difficult and obscure for a folk riddler to use.

Ibn Shabîn (1107–1175), also of Bagdad, was famous as the maker of insoluble riddles and the solver of all that were propounded to him. He enjoyed such a reputation that two of his friends, Abû Ghâleb ibn Ḥusain and Abû Mansûr ibn Sulaimân (1149–1224) of Samarkand, endeavored to defeat him. Riddling continued to flourish in the thirteenth century, and even as late as the beginning of the fifteenth the Egyptian Zain ad-Dîn ibn 'Ajmî (fl. 1409) wrote a riddle of the ringdove.[25] This long and complicated play on the words *fakhitatun* (dove), *fa-'ukhtun* (and the sister), *'akhun* (brother), and others of similar sound cannot be translated.

---

[24] *Ibid.*, III, no. 264.
[25] *Ibid.*, III, no. 283.

Other riddles in the *Majânî l'Adab* deserve to be quoted for the ingenuity of their conceptions or as parallels to the treatments of familiar themes. A riddle by Usama ibn Munqidh deals with the unusual subject of the extraction of a molar tooth:

> A friend, whose companionship is not lessened as time
>   goes on,
> Who is wretched and who exerts himself diligently so
>   that I should profit,
> In all the course of our being together I have never met
>   him
> And at the time when he appeared before my eyes
>   we parted forever.[26]

Sharaf ad-Daula's riddle of the wasp and the bee has the simplicity of a folk riddle:

> Both are singing and humming in a congregation
> And people will repel them because of their harmfulness.
> One gives bountifully of what the other gives nothing;
> This one is being praised while that one is being blamed.[27]

So, also, Abû Sarfin's description of a needle in terms suggesting a horse or camel is probably of popular inspiration:

> It has a fragile body,
> The work it does is for a strong purpose.
> Its hoof is in its head;
> Its eye is in its tail.[28]

---

[26] *Ibid.*, III, no. 265.
[27] *Ibid.*, II, no. 238.
[28] *Ibid.*, II, no. 231.

An anonymous riddle for fire contains only the themes found in folk riddles:

> Something that devours without mouth or stomach,
> Trees and animals are food for it.
> If you feed it, it becomes vigorous and lives;
> But if you give it a drink of water, it dies.[29]

Of the many riddles for a pen I select only one as an example of literary elaboration:

> It does not walk, no, but it is not lame.
> It has no head and no sensing hand.
> It is not alive, no, yet it is not dead.
> But it is a person seen in congregations,
> With a spittle more poisonous than that of a viper.
> It crawls stealthily in the depth of night;
> Because of its fearful silence it is most terrifying
> And it cuts the artery under the helmet.
> To the eye that beholds it its position appears very
>   low:
> It is impossible to spot this little inkspot among a
>   mass of unarranged things.[30]

Among all the many Arabic riddlemasters the one most easily available to a non-Arabist and also the most important is Al-Ḥarîrî of Bassorah, who was born soon after 1050 and lived the alloted three-score years and ten, dying not long after 1120. His *Assemblies* or *Maqâmât*, a classical work, includes several chapters of enigmas of one kind or another. An

---

[29] *Ibid.*, II, no. 291.
[30] *Ibid.*, III, no. 258. The last line involves a play on words that cannot be easily reproduced in English.

"assembly" is a literary form devised by Al-Hama-dhânî (d. 1008). "He imagined a witty, unscrupulous improviser, wandering from place to place and living on the presents which the display of his gifts produced from the generous and tasteful, and a kind of Râwi or narrator, who should be continually meeting with the other, should relate his adventures and repeat his excellent compositions. To these he gave the name of Makâmât, or 'Assemblies,' because the Improviser was always introduced as making his appearance in some company of strangers among whom the narrator happened to be, and as astonishing them by his rhetoric and poetry."[31]

Al-Ḥarîrî gives only one kind of enigma in an assembly. The Fifteenth Assembly relates a legal puzzle which asks and explains "how a man, dying childless, could leave a brother perfectly competent to inherit and yet that his property should go to his wife's brother." The Twenty-fourth Assembly contains questions about fine points in Arabic grammar and syntax. Like the English puzzle: "What English sentence cannot be printed?—There are three [tū]'s in the English language," they are intelligible only in the original. The Thirty-second Assembly deals with various legal complications, which often turn on a pun. The Thirty-sixth Assembly contains conundrums.

The most interesting of Al-Ḥarîrî's riddles remain to be mentioned. He described a flint in a series of

---

[31] Chenery and Steingass (trans.), *The Assemblies of Al-Ḥarîrî*, I, 19.

contradictions[32] as a modern riddler might do, and compared a wine cask to a maiden.[33] His riddle for a needle may have a foundation in folklore, but shows the elaboration characteristic of the literary artist. It is as follows:

Behold I had a slave girl, elegant of shape, smooth of cheek, patient to labour;—At one time she ambled like a good steed, at another she slept quietly in her bed: even in July thou wouldst feel her touch to be cool.—She had understanding and discretion, sharpness and wit, a hand with fingers, but a mouth without teeth; yet did she pique as with tongue of snake, and saunter in trailing robe; and she was displayed in blackness and whiteness; and she drank, but not from cisterns.—She was truth-telling, now beguiling, now hiding, peeping forth; yet fitted for employment, obedient in poverty and wealth: if thou didst spurn her, she showed affection, but if thou didst put her from thee, she remained quietly apart.—Generally would she serve thee, and be courteous to thee, though sometimes she might be froward to thee and pain thee, and trouble thee.[34]

---

[32] Twenty-ninth Assembly.

[33] Thirty-fifth Assembly.

[34] Chenery explains the application to a needle thus: "I had a needle, straight of shape and smooth of side, lasting for work; that sometimes moved quickly in the sewer's hands, and sometimes rested in the needle-box; it was sometimes filed in July, it had strength to hold with its rein of thread, it had sharpness and point; it hemmed the garment by the aid of the sewer's fingers; it had a mouth (eye) without teeth; it sometimes pricked with its point, as it was driven through the cloth; it carried a long thread after it; it had sometimes a black thread and sometimes a white thread; it was bedewed only with the sweat of the sewer's hand; it sewed the cloth or lined it; it now hid itself behind the cloth, and now appeared again; it was adapted for use; it went easily into any orifice, small or large; if thou didst rend anything, it joined it, but if thou didst lay it aside in the needle-box, it remained where it was put; mostly did it serve thee and adorn thee by its work, but sometimes it would prick thee, and pain thee and trouble thee." See Chenery and Steingass, I, 146–147.

It was quite natural that so useful a tool as the needle should find special favor among riddlemasters everywhere. The needle theme was especially popular in Italy, where we find many traditional and literary versions of it.[35] Catone l'Uticense (*Enimmi*, no. 71) uses it in the following sonnet:

> Preso ch'io sono, e steso mi tenete,
>> Subito a un non so che la punta fate,
>> Con cui qual Polifemo mi acciecate,
>> Sol per condurmi appunto ove volete.
>
> E mentre così a man mi conducete,
>> A forza d'urti, e spinte andar mi fate;
>> E dietro a me venir su mie pedate,
>> A quei, che m'acciecò sol permettete.
>
> Sia monte, o pian per dove vado, e passo,
>> Aspro e duro il sentier, o molle sia,
>> Rilevate sul suol l'orme mie lasso.
>
> Quei, che meco si mosse, per la via
>> Vien meno, e addietro resta; e pur con passo
>> Egual vien sempre meco in compagnia.

Although quite satisfactory artistically, this sonnet lacks the minute details and the elaborateness of the Arabic version. We see here the needle in action from the moment the sewer threads it, and we notice the impression the stitches create. The Italian octaves are

---

[35] Stigliani, *Rime*, p. 246, no. 18; Chiariti, *Enimmi*, p. 33, no. 86; Salani, *Raccolta*, p. 29, no. 54. All these are in octaves. Salani's *Raccolta* is not an original work, but is (as the title implies) gathered from various sources. I have not discovered where he found this needle riddle.

less elaborate; and hence they are also less confusing and perhaps more acceptable to the modern reader.

Al-Ḥarîrî's riddle for a loaf is of special interest because we shall find a similar conception in European riddling. He writes:

Take with thee the one of full-moon face and of pearly hue, of pure root and tormented body, who was pinched and stretched, imprisoned and released, made to drink and weaned, and pushed into the fire, after he had been slapped.[36]

Elsewhere he describes the koḥl pencil, used to blacken the eyelids:

What groom is it who weds, both in secret and openly, two sisters, and no offence at his wedlock is ever found?

When waiting on one, he waits as well on the other eke; if husbands are partial, no such bias is seen in him;

His attentions increase as the sweethearts are growing grey, and so does his largess: what a rare thing in married man![37]

The pen riddle also contains themes, doubtless of popular origin, which have parallels in Western tradition and literature. It is:

One split in his head it is through whom "the writ" is known, as honoured recording angels take their pride in him;

When given to drink he craves for more, as though athirst, and settles to rest when thirstiness takes hold of him;

---

[36] Chenery and Steingass, II, 16, Assembly 29. Most of the features present in this riddle will reappear in Italian versions; see De Filippis, pp. 22–23, 76, 85, 109–114.

[37] Chenery and Steingass, II, 116, Assembly 42.

And scatters tears about him when he bids him run, but tears that sparkle with the brightness of a smile.[38]

The last of Al-Ḥarîrî's riddles that I shall quote is that of the scales, which is also an elaboration of a popular theme:

One flighty and leaning with one half to one side, but no man of sense will upbraid him for either:

He is always raised up on high as a just king is rightly exalted for aye in his station.

Alike to him are both the pebble and the nugget, though truth should in no wise be balanced with falsehood.

And most to be wondered at in his description, if people regard him as with eyes of discernment,

Is that by his judgment the parties abide, though they know him as flighty by nature, and partial.[39]

The fundamental themes of these and the remaining riddles composed by Al-Ḥarîrî are popular, but the elaboration, which often goes very far, is his own.

In his Introduction to a translation of Al-Ḥarîrî's *Assemblies*, Chenery[40] directs attention to their "great influence," but does not make clear whether such imitations as the fifty assemblies composed by Abû ṭ-Ṭâhir Moḥammad ibn Yusuf of Cordova (d. 1143), or the similar modern book by Nâṣif al-Yâziji, a

---

[38] Chenery and Steingass, II, 116, Assembly 42. The pen is especially popular in Italy, and we have literary versions of it by Cenni (*Sonetti*, no. 2), Straparola (*Notti*, VI, 1; VIII, 3), Croce (*Notte sollazzevole*, I, no. 28), Chiariti (*Enimmi*, no. 86), Catone l'Uticense (*Enimmi*, no. 98). In others it appears indirectly under Inkwell, Writing, etc. Popular versions are even more numerous.

[39] Chenery and Steingass, II, 118, Assembly 42.

[40] Chenery and Steingass, I, 97–98.

Christian Arab of Beirout, contain riddles. Gustav
Rosen translated some very difficult Arabic riddles
involving the meanings of words or grammatical
subtleties.[41] The enigmatic art has long been popular
among writers of Arabic, but rather few examples
have been translated into western European languages.[42] Some riddles found in stories in the *Arabian
Nights* will be mentioned in another connection.[43]

Hebrew riddling has a long history,[44] but we shall
not start here with Samson's question[45] with which he
confused the Philistines at his wedding. This special
variety of folk riddle sets a puzzle that no one can
guess because the event described is known only to
the speaker. Since an exercise of wits was appropriate
to a wedding in Palestine—and since it has long continued to be customary on such occasions,—we can
infer that many examples of this widely practiced art
have been lost to us. Some have seen a riddle in the
Nineteenth Psalm, but thus to interpret the passage
seems forced. The King James Version of the Bible

---

[41] See "Proben neuerer gelehrter Dichtkunst der Araber," *Zeitschrift
der Deutschen morgenländischen Gesellschaft,* XIII (1859), 249–255; XIV
(1860), 692–705; XX (1866), 589–595; and XXII (1868), 541–544.

[42] See Carl Brockelmann, *Geschichte der arabischen Literatur,* passim.

[43] See p. 41 below.

[44] See Friedreich, pp. 157–163; Israel Abrahams, *Jewish Life in the
Middle Ages* (New York, 1907), p. 386; Joseph Jacobs, *Jewish Ideals*
(London, 1896), p. 108, and article, "Riddle," *Jewish Encyclopedia,* X
(New York, 1905), 408–409; Jefim Schirman, "Rätsel," *Jüdisches Lexi-
kon,* IV (Berlin, 1930), cols. 1252–1253. August Wünsche, *Die Rätsel-
weisheit bei den alten Hebräern mit Hinblick auf andere alte Völker* (Leipzig,
1883), and Harry Torczyner, "The Riddle in the Bible," *Hebrew Union
College Annual,* I (1924), 125–150, deal exclusively with riddles in the
Old Testament.

[45] Judges, 14: 12–14.

calls the allegorical passage in Ezekiel, 17: 3–10 a riddle or parable, but in doing so it extends the term "riddle" beyond its ordinary use. The description of old age in Ecclesiastes, 12:2–6 is more properly regarded as a riddle, but since it lacks some formal characteristics of the type I shall not insist upon including it here.[46] Simeon ben Ḥalafta, who lived not long after A.D. 220, used a similar theme as an excuse for not paying a call when he wrote: "Rocks have become high [he was growing old]; the near are at a distance [his eyesight was dim]; two are turned into three [he walked with a cane]: and the peacemaker of the home has ceased [he could no longer exercise his functions]."[47] A Talmudic riddle for an ibis, "What animal has one voice living and seven voices dead?" which refers to the seven different musical instruments made from the bird's body, belongs to the folk pattern rather than to literature.[48] An early poetic riddle in the Talmud Yerushalmi gives a variety of details but no answer, and the commentators have not agreed on supplying the missing link. The text reads as follows:

> High from heav'n her eye looks down,
> Consistent strife excites her frown,

---

[46] See Torczyner, pp. 136–137; Denis Buzy, C.S.J., "Le Portrait de la vieillesse," *Revue biblique*, XLI (1932), 329–340.

[47] The tractate Shabbath in the Babylonian Talmud, fol. 152a. See August Wünsche, *Der babylonische Talmud*, I, i (Leipzig, 1886), 173; Isidore Epstein (ed.), *The Babylonian Talmud: Seder Mo'ed*, II (London, 1938), 776.

[48] At the end of the tractate Kinnim in the Babylonian Talmud; see Wünsche, II, iv (Leipzig, 1889), 170.

> Wingèd beings shun her sight,
> She puts the youth to constant flight,
> The aged, too, her looks do scout,
> "Oh! Oh!," the fugitive cries out,
> And by her snares whoe'er is lured
> Can never of his sin be cured.[49]

In the tenth century, Dunash ben Labrat, the founder of Spanish Hebrew poetry, wrote riddles.[50] Although his verses and those of his contemporaries were praised in the next century, they were so much obscured by the refined and exquisite poetry of a new school in the twelfth century that his riddles disappeared from sight and have only recently been recovered. Nehemya Aluny has identified and printed ten of Dunash ben Labrat's riddles and cites others in manuscripts in New York and Leningrad that can be assigned to him with greater or less probability. These riddles occupy a very important place chronologically in the history of literary riddling, since they stand midway between the abundant Latin and Old English riddling of the seventh and eighth centuries and a second flourishing of the art in the Middle Ages. I do not, however, perceive any close connection in subject matter between them and either the earlier or the subsequent flowering. From a translation of Dunash ben Labrat's riddles generously made for me by my colleague, Professor Walter J. Fischel, I select the fol-

---

[49] Quoted from the *Jewish Encyclopedia*, X, 409.
[50] Nehemya Aluny, "Ten [of] Dunash ben Labrat's Riddles," *Jewish Quarterly Review*, XXXVI (1945–1946), 141–146.

lowing examples. All are in distichs in the conventional *wâfir* meter. Although the answers are lacking and must be supplied by conjecture, most of the themes are clear enough.

Dunash ben Labrat describes a watermelon in the following terms:

There is a box that is not full and not empty and all the boxes are created. It has black daughters and also reddish ones and they are covered with a greenish handkerchief.

The distich

What speaks in all languages in his riding, and his mouth spits the poison of life or death? It is silent when it rests, and is deaf like a boy or one of the poor

clearly refers to a pen. Dunash ben Labrat intended a candle when he wrote:

What weeps tears without an eye, and makes everything visible and does not see its own garment; at the time when it approaches its death that which cuts off its head revives it?

The subjects of Dunash ben Labrat's riddles and the details found in them suggest that he versified folk themes. He also ventured into the field of abstract ideas, which are frequently used in literary riddles and only rarely in folklore. For

And my son explained to me what maidens are never carrying on incest. They are beautiful and good altogether, hidden like closed gardens,

the commentators suggest the answer "new ideas." Since these riddles have a position of strategic importance, a critical edition of Dunash ben Labrat based on the several available manuscripts is greatly to be desired. 1147785

Although literary riddling was actively practiced in Spain in the eleventh century and later, it is difficult to learn much about it. Moses ibn Ezra, who was born at Granada about 1070 and died after 1138, was a writer of riddles. His candle riddle, "What is the sister of the sun, though made for the night? The fire causes her tears to fall, and when she is near dying they cut off her head,"[51] uses folk themes and also shows a literary elaboration surpassing that of Dunash ben Labrat. Abraham ibn Ezra (1092/1093-1167), a member of the same family, was a little younger than his friend Jehuda Halevi. He was the author of grammatical riddles and enigmas on the letters *mem* and *nun*. We can infer that he was influenced by contemporary Arabic riddling on similar themes. Al-Ḥarîzî, who flourished at the beginning of the thirteenth century, is frequently referred to as a writer of riddles. Only the first twenty-six and part of the twenty-seventh assemblies of his translation of Al-Ḥarîrî's *Maqâmât* have been preserved, and this portion (at least in the Arabic original) contains only one riddle, a legal problem in the fifteenth assembly. Nevertheless, the *Tachkemoni*, an original work similar to Al-Ḥarîrî's *Maqâmât*, mentions in several places that it contains riddles, though the pertinent passages have not been translated.

---

[51] Quoted from the *Jewish Encyclopedia*, X, 409.

Although a good deal of Jehuda Halevi's poetry has been translated, only a few of his riddles are available to those who cannot read Hebrew. Jehuda Halevi (b. 1085 or 1086 in Castille, d. after 1140) is one of the major medieval lyric poets and perhaps the most important writer of the time to compose riddles. His description of a grain of wheat contains themes found in folk riddles. It is as follows: "What is it that one lays naked in the grave and yet it does not suffer death, it begets children there, it cares for them attentively, until they appear fully dressed?"[52] The details of his description of a pen occur again and again in later literary and semiliterary texts and give an idea of the materials available to the early versifiers of this theme. Halevi's version cannot be rated as particularly successful, for it exhibits the usual fault of literary riddling: it confuses themes belonging to entirely different conceptions of the object. The text is as follows:

A little staff, yet of inestimable value, green in color as if consumed by love-sorrow, a hollow body yet with a brave heart, it casts down heroes, it brings pain to many, it hastens to fill itself[53] properly, it does not accomplish its task with empty mouth. And five servants are ready at one time, cheerfully executing its commands. Now it likes to communicate song and elegance, now it is able to soften a prince's heart, it can make peace, it can bring about war. Tell what it is, what it means.

---

[52] This and the following riddles by Jehuda Halevi are translated from the German versions in Friedreich, pp. 157–158.
[53] I have emended *sie* (it, her, them) to *sich* (itself).

Jehuda Halevi's riddle for the sky when rain is needed employs the contradictions characteristic of popular riddling but develops them in a literary manner: "What is it, then, at which our heart laughs merrily when it weeps, but makes our heart sad and mournful when it shines brightly?" The theme reminds me of Till Eulenspiegel, who is said always to have wept when going downhill because he knew an ascent would follow, and to have laughed merrily on climbing a hill because he anticipated the descent sure to come.

Nor was the writing of Hebrew riddles limited to Spain in the Middle Ages. Immanuel ben Solomon ben Jekuthiel (Immanuel of Rome), who lived from 1265 to 1330 and had some interesting connections with Dante that do not now concern us, wrote Hebrew poetry in the style of Al-Ḥarîrî's *Maqâmât*. He is also credited with the authorship of a long verse riddle having the answer "matter." As we can guess from its subject, it is difficult to solve and has been called pedantic by some. Finally, at the very end of the period that we are considering, Israel Onceneyra (fl. 1577) carried the Spanish art of riddling to Turkey.[54] In view of the interest and importance of Hebrew riddling, it is to be hoped that a competent Hebraist will write an account of its long and curious history.

Although riddling flourished in Turkey, I have not been able to learn much more than the names of

---

[54] *Jüdisches Lexikon*, IV, col. 1253.

those who practiced it.[55] 'Alî, an itinerant seller of leeches, who was called Mamāji (the enigmatic one), gained fame for his skill in setting and guessing riddles and composed a treatise on the subject. The dervish poet Maḥmûd ibn Othmân ibn 'Alî Nakkāsh (d. 938), who was known as Lami'î (the brilliant), wrote various riddles. From the six that are accessible I select his description of a spoon:

Tell me on what branch the bird is singing?—The bird which, light as a feather, has wings of silver, and whenever it flies merrily back and forth, plunges like a boat into the sea, and whenever it rises, always bears a load of fruit in its beak. It flies up to a nest of rubies, in which a parrot is confined. It gives the morsel to the parrot and returns. That is its daily activity with good cheer. After he has told this to strangers, Lâmi'î may well ask for an answer.

Fāni, a spice merchant, who lived about 1003, may have been inspired by this to write his riddles comparing the lips of his sweetheart to a ruby cup filled with pearls. Surûrî, who has been called the Turkish Boileau, is said to have discussed the rules of riddling.

In Persian literature the most famous riddles are perhaps those asked by the hero Zāl in Firdūsi's epic, the *Shahnameh*. Firdūsi, who was born in 940, tells

---

[55] Friedreich, pp. 163–166, citing Joseph Hammer-Purgstall, *Geschichte der osmanischen Dichtkunst*, II (Pest, 1837). Some of these authors will be found in E. J. W. Gibb, *A History of Ottoman Literature* (6 vols., London, 1901–1907), where their interest in riddling is dealt with briefly, if at all. We have not identified 'Alî and Fāni. Surûrî may have lived in the sixteenth century, but the identification is uncertain. Friedreich is quoting here Joseph Hammer-Purgstall, *Geschichte der schönen Redekünste Persiens* (Vienna, 1818), p. 34.

how Zal appeared before Manōtshihr, the emperor of Iran. The emperor was frightened and planned to get Zal out of the way. After his counselors advised him that Zal would become an unparalleled hero with a boundless love for Iran, the emperor accepted Zal and tested him with riddles. The themes are cosmological. Typical are the riddles for the year,

Twelve cypresses stand in a circle and shine in resplendent green; each has thirty branches, and neither their esteem nor their number becomes less in the land of the Parsees,

the day and night,

There are two splendid horses, one black as pitch, the other of shining crystal; each runs ahead of the other but never catches it,

and an elaborate literary allegory of the world,

There is a green garden full of birds; a man with a large scythe goes about it, busily mowing green and dry plants; neither complaints nor submission to his will divert him from his purpose. There two cypresses rise from the waves of the sea like reeds; a bird has its nest in them. When it is sitting in them, there is a fragrance like musk. One of the trees is always green and bears fruit, the other is wilting.— The two halves of heaven (cypresses), the sun (bird), the zodiacal sign of the ram (nest), death.

Firdūsi is the best known and most easily accessible writer of Persian riddles, but many of his contemporaries of the tenth and eleventh centuries also practiced the art.[56] Only fragments now exist of the writings of Asjadi of Merv, a poet of the court of Sultan Maḥmûd, but among them is the following riddle for a melon:

> Color, taste, and fragrance: emeralds, sugar, and musk;
> Amber for the tongue, colored matter for the eye.
> If you split it, each split portion duplicates the new
>   moon.
> If you leave it whole, it represents the full moon.[57]

Rāzi, who is also known as Abû-l Mufachir, is said to have founded Persian riddling, but he is clearly a generation or two later than Firdūsi.[58] Watwât, who lived from 1088 to 1182, is said to have discussed riddles in his handbook of poetics. A second group of riddlers belongs to a time about three centuries later. The historian Sheref-ed-dîn 'Ali of Yezd (d. 1430), who wrote the life of Tamerlane, is credited with some riddles. In the following century the emir Khānzāde, who was called Tablbas (the drummer) and Deliri (the latter was his name as a poet), and Maulana Nisan of Astrabad (d. 1515) wrote others. Unfortunately none of these have been put into a European language and historians of Persian literature have shown almost no interest in them.

As a conclusion to this brief review of Oriental riddling we may mention some very famous and widely

---

[56] I follow here Friedreich, pp. 166–167.

[57] See Friedreich, p. 167, where this quatrain is quoted from J. Hammer-Purgstall, *Geschichte der schönen Redekünste Persiens*, p. 44.

[58] See also Hammer-Purgstall, *ibid.*, p. 79.

circulated stories containing riddles. Such typically Oriental stories have arisen in various forms and at various times in the early Middle Ages, or even earlier, from Persia to Greece and have often been carried westward in later centuries. They tell of a contest between a learned man and a girl or a slave who displays a surprising wit and surpasses an opponent.[59] A widely known version of this theme is the *Historia della Donzella Theodor*, which was printed in Spain in the fifteenth century and is supposed to be much older.[60] It is closely related to the story of Tawaddud, which is found first in eighteenth century manuscripts of the *Arabian Nights*.[61] From Persia the story of Turandot found its way through the *Arabian Nights* to modern Italy and Germany.[62] Carlo Gozzi and Schiller took pleasure in rewriting the riddles for modern ears. Schiller had so keen an interest in puzzling his audience that he composed new texts for use after the first night. In these framework stories such variations and modernizations are frequent. They are especially noteworthy in the late Greek romance of Apollonius of Tyre, in which the riddles change greatly as the story is carried about. The riddles in the legend of Aḥiḳar, a very old and famous Levan-

[59] For discussion of this theme see Jan de Vries, *Die Märchen von den klugen Rätsellösern* ("FF Communications," LXXIII, Helsinki, 1928); Albert Wesselski, "Die gelehrten Sklavinnen und ihre byzantinischen Vorbilder," *Archiv orientální*, IX (1937), 333-378.

[60] Walther Suchier, *L'Enfant sage*, pp. 125-131, 158-163, 191-222, 395-405.

[61] See Wesselski, pp. 357 ff., and Victor Chauvin, *Bibliographie des ouvrages arabes*, VII (Liége, 1903), 117-118.

[62] Chauvin, *Bibliographie*, V, 195.

tine story, also vary considerably from text to text.[63] Framework tales of the kinds just described made a substantial contribution to the art of writing literary riddles. The themes of these riddles are usually taken from folklore, and the hand of the literary artist is evident in their elaboration.

We turn now to Greece, where riddling has flourished from the beginning of literary history.[64] The riddle of the Sphinx is an ancient puzzle; and tradition relates that Homer himself died from vexation at failing to guess a riddle for lice. Although scholars studied riddles in classical times, their works are now lost and we are limited to what Athenaeus[65] tells us. These early riddles are of the popular sort, and we need only note that they were on occasion elaborated by literary men.

There are two sources of Greek literary riddles: the Greek Anthology and Byzantine literature. The fourteenth book of the Greek Anthology contains many riddles by authors of various periods. Some are simple epigrams in the folk spirit and doubtless of folk origin; others are highly sophisticated inventions. There are also arithmetical puzzles, which we can pass over here as a form of little importance in the history of literary riddling. Typical of the simpler riddles is one for smoke: "I am the black child of a white father, a

---

[63] Chauvin, *Bibliographie*, VI, 40.

[64] See Ohlert, *Rätsel und Rätselspiele der alten Griechen*. The first edition (Berlin, 1886) is somewhat fuller in comparisons and criticism than the second edition (Berlin, 1912). See also the treatise by Lilio Gregorio Giraldi cited below, p. 73.

[65] *Deipnosophistae*, Book X.

wingless bird, flying even to the clouds of heaven. I
give birth to tears of mourning in pupils that meet
me, and at once on my birth I am dissolved in air."[66]
The conception occurs again and again in folk riddles
for smoke, and the contrast of black and white is also
a favorite popular theme. The confused suggestion of
both a person and a bird is a fault often found in
literary riddling. In Italy there are several literary
versions of this riddle. Croce (*Notte sollazzevole*, I, no.
24, p. 282) treats it thus:

> Pria di mia madre nasco, nè sì tosto
>   son nato, ch'io mi pongo per camino;
>   e da la terra tanto mi discosto,
>   che passo de le nubi ogni confino;
>   e d'una tal maniera son composto,
>   che non hò corpo, e pur qual pellegrino
>   vagando vò pe 'l mondo notte, e giorno,
>   e nel loco, ov'io nasco, mai non torno.

The only resemblance here to the Greek version is line
four, which is very close to "flying even to the clouds
of heaven." Chiariti (*Enimmi*, no. 36, p. 17) in his
version emphasizes the uselessness of the smoke by
comparing it with the splendor of fire and the useful-
ness of the other things connected with it:

> Mio padre vive al mondo con splendore
>   Essendo corteggiato da più gente,
>   La mia Sorella e 'l mio fratel minore
>   Servon quando n'è il tempo ogni vivente,

---

[66] XIV, 5. The word here translated pupils signifies both 'girls' and the
'pupils of the eyes.'

> Ed io misero me come il peggiore
> Di tutti, non essendo buon da niente,
> Abborrito da tutti son forzato
> Con mio gran biasmo a tor dall 'uom comiato.

Catone l'Uticense (*Enimmi*, no. 26) has elaborated it into a sonnet which fuses together most of the features present in the other versions:

> Di chiaro Genitor, di gran lignaggio
> Figlio ignobil son io vile, e sprezzato.
> Col Padre a un tempo nasco, e appena nato
> In cammino mi pongo, ed in viaggio.
>
> Essendo a questo avvezzo, è poco saggio
> Quei, che in casa mi tien chiuso, e serrato,
> Che tosto agli occhi suoi m'avvento irato,
> Sì che altrove fuggendo ei fa passaggio.
>
> In ogni casa a me s'alza, e s'appresta
> Il baldacchino; onde a ragione approvo,
> Se superbo si tien quei, che m'ha in testa.
>
> Fra molti vizj miei solo mi resta
> Questo di buon, che sempre mi ritrovo
> A la Messa, ed al Vespro i dì di Festa.

A description of the double flute by Athenaeus, "One wind, two ships, ten sailors rowing, and one steersman directs both,"[67] has the simplicity of the folk riddle. The riddle for silence, "Speak not and thou shalt speak my name. But must thou speak? Thus again, a great marvel, in speaking thou shalt speak my name,"[68] shows some literary elaboration, but contains a theme

---

[67] XIV, 14.   [68] XIV, 22.

found in such a modern American riddle as "What is that which if you name it you break it?" In "From the sea I have a fishy parentage, and one contest can bring me to the games of Dionysus. In the stadium, after anointing my body with oil, I slew by my hands the son of Demeter. In the second place, I send out from both sides of me a mass of giants, pulled by my hands,"[69] the inventor has so completely disguised the answer that no one has guessed it. These examples will sufficiently illustrate the epigrams of the Greek Anthology and the popularity of riddling in ancient Greece. In the Renaissance, writers accepted the Anthology as a model and rewrote some of its riddles.[70]

At Byzantium or under its influence the writing of literary riddles extended from the first half of the tenth to the end of the thirteenth century.[71] The earliest of these riddles are unsophisticated and apparently casual versifications of folk themes. In later times, that is, from the latter part of the eleventh through a climax in the twelfth and to a close at the

---

[69] XIV, 28.

[70] See James Hutton, *The Greek Anthology in Italy to the Year 1800* ("Cornell Studies in English," XXIII, Ithaca, 1931) and *The Greek Anthology in France and in the Latin Writers of the Netherlands to the Year 1800* ("Cornell Studies," XXVIII, Ithaca, 1946).

[71] I rely upon Karl Krumbacher, *Geschichte der byzantinischen Literatur* (2d ed., Munich, 1897); Johann Albert Fabricius, *Bibliotheca graeca* (ed. Harles; Hamburg, 1790–1809), *passim*; Karl Dilthey, "Symbolae criticae ad Anthologiam graecam ex libris manuscriptis petitae," *Index lectionum für das Sommersemester, 1891* (Göttingen, 1891), pp. 6–18; G. S. Destunis, "Ocherki grecheskoi zagadki s drevnikh vremen do novykh," *Zhurnal ministerstva narodnago prosvescheniia*, CCLXX (1890), 66–98, 262–290. Many of the pertinent texts will be found in J. F. Boissonade, *Anecdota graeca e codicibus regiis*, III (Paris, 1831), 429–455.

end of the thirteenth century, poetasters and men active in ecclesiastical and political affairs developed and maintained a tradition of literary riddling much as we might find a similar tradition of limerick writing in modern times. The style was highly artificial and the subjects were, except when taken from the folk, abstract. The history of this literary tradition is not very well known, and I can only indicate its high points.

A description of salt by Johannes Kipriotes, who was born in the first half of the tenth century, is perhaps the oldest Byzantine riddle. Its author, who is usually called Johannes Geometres for his mathematical studies, won fame by epigrams and occasional poems. Krumbacher,[72] whose exact knowledge of Byzantine literature commands admiration, regards Johannes Geometres as one of the most interesting of all Byzantine writers. Unfortunately he does not say whether Johannes wrote more riddles.

The second Byzantine riddler, Christophorus of Mytilene, flourished in the first half of the eleventh century. It does not appear how many riddles he composed, and we may have lost some. Krumbacher,[73] who rates Christophorus among the best Byzantine poets, singles out for special praise his verses on some annoying mice. The fact that mice later destroyed his poems is an amusing instance of unconscious poetic prophecy. Krumbacher translates a riddle for snow as

[72] Krumbacher, pp. 734–737, sec. 306.
[73] Krumbacher, pp. 737–740, sec. 307.

an example of the poet's skill: "You seized me and
yet I fled; you see me flee and cannot hold me tight;
you press me in your hand but I escape and your fist
is left empty." The verses are the work of Christophorus, but the theme is ultimately of popular origin.
In Italy, literary versions of the snow riddle may be
found in almost every collection. Catone l'Uticense's
version (*Enimmi*, no. 138) is of special interest because its second quatrain is very similar to Christophorus' conception:

> Sappi, se mia beltà tanto t'alletta,
>> Che altrettanto rigore a quella unisco;
>> Quindi non preme a me d'esser negletto
>> Per le contrade, quando fuor sortisco.
>
> Con chi più m'accarezza, io più infierisco;
>> E chi mi vuol tener più forte, e stretta,
>> Da le man più gli fuggo, e gli sparisco:
>> Che il trattenermi al dipartir m'affretta.
>
> Ne le risoluzion mie sempre ondeggio,
>> Nè stabil son a cui m'appiglio; e allora
>> Vie più, se un tal, per cui languisco, io veggio.
>
> Il tempo, ch'ogni cosa al fin divora,
>> In mia madre mi cangia: e quel ch'è peggio,
>> Viva sepolta son perch'io non mora.

A third Byzantine writer of riddles, Johannes Mau-
ropus, follows almost immediately upon Christophorus of Mytilene.[74] He seems to have begun to write
about 1050. Nothing much is said about his riddles.

[74] Krumbacher, pp. 740–742, sec. 308; Fabricius, ed. Harles, VIII,
627–633.

One of the best-known Byzantine riddlemasters is Michael Psellus, an encyclopedist and statesman, who flourished in the last quarter of the eleventh century.[75] He, too, appears to have employed folk themes, as we can infer from this riddle for scales: "I am justice. I am the height of justice. I have six ribs, but only two legs."[76] The six ribs are the cords holding the pans of the scales. Other Oriental riddles compare scales to a judge whose decisions all accept. One Italian example, Catone l'Uticense's (*Enimmi*, no. 56), will suffice to give us a clear idea of how such a theme may be artistically elaborated:

> Alza sopra d'un palco (udite attenti)
>   Un Giudice severo il Tribunale.
>   E di Regi, e Monarchi in dì fatale
>   Esamina a minuto i mancamenti.
>
> Del suo strano rigor odo portenti;
>   Difetti i più leggier, come gran male
>   Più castiga: ed i rei con pena eguale
>   Tien sospesi a tortura, e gl'innocenti.
>
> Tra quei, che contro lor son testimonj,
>   De la terra è un gran figlio (e vel ripeto)
>   Che si corrompe sì, ma non co i doni.
>
> Del Giudice ecco al fin quel sì gran zelo
>   Di giustizia sì retta: i giusti, e buoni
>   Manda a l'Inferno, e i più cattivi al Cielo.

---

[75] Krumbacher, p. 444, sec. 184, 4; Boissonade, III, 429–436.

[76] Boissonade, III, no. 15. Basil Megalomites has the same riddle with a single word changed (see Boissonade, no. 26), and Hilberg reports an anonymous version; see his p. 214, no. 11.

More than a score of riddles by Basilios Megalomites, who was writing not long after Psellus, have been
printed. Since the greater part of them employ the
device of omitting or inserting letters to indicate the
answer, translation is impossible. His riddle for a
letter (*epistola*) is a repetition of a similar riddle used
by the comedian Antiphanes in his *Sappho* of the late
fourth century B.C. Basilios writes as follows: "There
is a vociferous and talkative feminine creature that
hides and guards its young in her bosom; the young
have no voices and are not taught to speak; nevertheless their speech is clear and loud, they talk to whom-
soever they like, even on the waters of the sea; they
reach those who live on islands and on the continent;
many of them, though present, cannot be heard. The
little ones cannot hear."[77] His very curious riddle for
a cock is nothing less than a comparison to a demon:
"There is such a male as the one who came out of a
white stone; at a distance his beard sparkles like
flame; the earth trembles under his feet; when he
cries out, the devils run for shelter; a gust of wind
comes from under his wings."[78] Yet this is clearly the
bird of dawning.

Krumbacher passes hastily over the riddles of
Theodorus Prodromus, who probably died in 1159.
We, too, must be brief. Although Prodromus always

[77] See Boissonade, III, 450–451, no. 39. The last line contains an error
of some sort. Antiphanes attributes deafness to those who do not understand what they read.

[78] See Boissonade, III, 445, no. 23. Krumbacher does not discuss
Basilius Megalomites. The cock was a favorite subject among Italian
riddlers; see De Filippis, pp. 55–57.

complained of poverty and constantly sought a patron even in unbecoming ways, he found opportunity —and it was perhaps because of his poverty—to write in almost every genre known in Byzantium. He wrote novels, occasional verse, epigrams, astrological, grammatical, philosophical, and theological works, and satires, orations, and letters. His riddles must be regarded as an employment of a genre flourishing at the time. Prodromus has usually been considered typical of the worst faults of Byzantine literature. Yet, as Krumbacher points out, he deserves fuller interpretation than he has received. Critics have displayed no interest in his riddles, and we must content ourselves with noting that he followed a prevailing fashion.[79]

Eleven riddles by Eustathius Makrembolites can now, after a long period of uncertainty, be safely dated in the last half of the twelfth century.[80] These sophisticated and artificial inventions contain manipulations of the answers in which letters are added, omitted, or altered. Such tricks have no trace of the folk in them. Eustathius has a better claim to fame as the author of a novel about Ismene and Ismenias, which was published twice in German in the last half of the seventeenth century. A recollection of it survived in a song which Goethe found in Alsace when he was

---

[79] Krumbacher, pp. 749–760, sec. 313, esp. p. 755.

[80] See Krumbacher, pp. 764–766, sec. 319. Eustathius is the only Byzantine riddlemaster who has had a modern critical edition. See M. Treu, *Eustathii Macrembolitae quae feruntur aenigmata* (Breslau, 1893), and the important review by I. Hilberg, *Byzantinische Zeitschrift*, III (1894), 172–175.

collecting folk songs for Herder. "Ich liebte nur Is-
menen" was, he complained, the only song that he
could find. Eustathius' riddles neither enjoyed so long
a life nor deserved such acclaim.

Aulikalamus,[81] who wrote only five riddles, was
probably a contemporary of Eustathius. His riddles
exhibit the same rhetorical manipulations of the
answers.

Nikephorus Prosuch,[82] a grandson of a Turkish
general, wrote metrical solutions of Aulikalamus' riddles. He seems also to have written some of his own.
He is supposed to have died about 1183.

The last Byzantine writer of riddles who is known
by name is Manuel Moschopulus, who lived during
the reign of Emperor Andronikus II Palaeologus
(1282-1328). Krumbacher remarks that his riddles
survive "in countless manuscripts," but modern
readers can learn little about them.[83]

Several anonymous collections which may belong
to the heyday of Byzantine riddling in the twelfth
century should be mentioned. They have been printed
in rare Greek journals for literature and folklore.[84]

---

[81] The riddles are printed in Boissonade, *Anecdota graeca*, III, 453-454.
Destunis mentions him several times, but Krumbacher does not give him
more than passing notice.

[82] Krumbacher, pp. 761-762, sec. 316. Prosuch was discovered by M.
Treu, who has printed all that has survived of his writings; see *Eustathii
Makrembolitae quae feruntur aenigmata*, pp. 10-14, 33-47.

[83] Krumbacher, pp. 546-548, sec. 224. For the riddles see Dilthey, 1891,
pp. 16-17.

[84] The first important collection of this sort was printed in 1877 (see
Krumbacher, p. 766, sec. 319, 5). For a list of such collections see Archer
Taylor, *A Bibliography of Riddles* ("FF Communications," CXXVI,
Helsinki, 1939), pp. 81-83.

During the last two generations a rather large number of such texts have seen the light, and the time is ripe for gathering and winnowing the harvest.

In western Europe, literary riddling began with the hundred Latin riddles of Symphosius.[85] We have no better authority for his name than an ascription in medieval manuscripts, and we know nothing about him beyond what can be inferred from a brief and uninformative prologue to his collection. The dates for this riddlemaster are quite uncertain, but are fixed, with some degree of probability, at the end of the fifth century.

For more than a thousand years Symphosius has been a model for writers of riddles, as Martial has been for writers of epigrams. He inspired the Anglo-Latin riddlers of the seventh and eighth centuries and through them the author of the Old English riddles in the *Exeter Book*.[86] Aldhelm acknowledged Symphosius to be his master and drew freely on him. Alcuin paraphrased seven Symphosian riddles in the *Disputatio regalis iuvenis Pippini cum Albino scholastico*.[87] No fewer than ten of them were used in the medieval versions of the *Historia Apollonii regis Tyri*,

---

[85] I follow the excellent critical comment in Tupper, *The Riddle of the Exeter Book*, pp. xxviii–xxx, and Ohl, *The Enigmas of Symphosius* (Diss.; Philadelphia, 1928). The latter gives a reliable edition, a translation, and an exhaustive bibliography.

[86] See especially Tupper, *Exeter Book*, *passim*.

[87] Wilhelm Wilmanns, *Zeitschrift für deutsches Altertum*, XIV (1869), 530. The riddles are Symphosius, nos. 75, 30, 14, 98, 99, 13, and 96. It is of some interest to note that no. 96, which is generally regarded as spurious, was present in its modern version in the collection known to Alcuin in the eighth century.

a romance which goes back to the seventh century.[88] Johann Camerarius (1500–1574) translated seventeen into Greek in his *Elementa Rhetoricae* (1545), a handbook[89] which was printed again in 1551, 1564, and 1600. These Greek riddles were also printed in Reusner's *Aenigmatographia*, an anthology of humanistic riddling. The riddles of Symphosius are excerpted for school use in the anonymous *Aenigmata et griphi veterum et recentium*,[90] published at Douai in 1604. Some of them may even be found in the anthology made by Franciscus a S. Barbara a century later, but they are no longer identified by the author's name.[91] After this time, we have found no indication that they were used in schools.

The long-enduring influence of Symphosius is most readily seen in the choice of one hundred for the number of riddles. Anglo-Latin and Old English riddlers strove to attain that number. The lost *Centiloquium aenigmatum* of Johannes Noblet,[92] which was written about 1430 and, to name no others, William Bellamy's *A Century of Charades*[93] in our own day are examples of this tradition.

In his prefatory remarks Symphosius does not find

---

[88] Ohl, p. 21. The riddles (found in *Historia*, chaps. 42, 43) are, in order, nos. 12, 2, 13, 89, 61, 63, 59, 69, 77, and 78. The choice of riddles varies greatly in the many versions of the Apollonius romance. See R. W. Pettengill, *Journal of English and Germanic Philology*, XII (1913), 248–251.

[89] See Ohl, p. 5.

[90] Unknown to Ohl. A copy in Archer Taylor's library.

[91] See p. 93, n. 175.

[92] See below, p. 72.

[93] Boston, 1896.

occasion to tell where he found his riddles. He does say, in a passage which the editors have deleted as spurious, that they were told at the Saturnalia. Even if we cannot claim this remark for Symphosius, we can cite it as evidence that, like Straparola and others, later copyists connected riddles with the carnival spirit.

As an example of a folk riddle versified by Symphosius we may note the following description of a snail:

> Porto domo mecum, semper migrare parata,
> Mutatoque solo non sum miserabilis exul,
> Sed mihi concilium de caelo nascitur ipso.[94]

Croce's version (*Notte sollazzevole*, I, no. 46, p. 284):

> Hò quattro corna à guisa di montone,
>   le quali or slungo, or scorto al mio comando
>   nè mai mi parto de la mia magione,
>   e pur sovente vò pe 'l mondo errando;
>   e si mì piace la mia habitatione,
>   ch'ovunque vado il tetto vo portando,
>   e se nel foco son gittata à sorte
>   canto, qual Cigno, la mia dolce morte,

enumerates the obvious characteristics of the snail: its perfect command over its four horns, and the fact that it carries a roof with it in its peregrinations.

---

94 No. 18. The last line has greatly troubled the editors (see Ohl, who collected the suggested readings). It seems to mean clearly enough: "But this wisdom is born of Heaven itself." *Concilium* is *consilium*, as often. Heaven gives me the ideas of bearing my house with me and of being always ready to move.

What is new in Croce's conception of the snail are the ideas that, like the swan, it sings when it is thrown into the fire, and that although it never leaves the house, it often wanders about the world. Michelangelo Buonarroti il Giovane has two short but original versions (*Indovinelli*, nos. 50 and 60, pp. 398, 400). The first reads thus:

> Io porto sempre una scala addosso,
>   Ma senza adoperarla, in alto ascendo;
>   E senza piedi ogni erto cammin prendo
>   (Gran cosa!), e ho le polpe dentro all'osso.

The things mentioned in this riddle are: the shell, which here becomes an ornamental ladder, never used by the snail in its painfully slow ascensions; the idea that it can climb without feet; and the additional idea that its flesh is within the bone. The second version is simpler and is more like an enigmatic question than a real riddle. In it we are simply asked to identify a harmless animal that, either through fear or anger, shuns caresses:

> Qual animal (o sia paura o ira)
>   È che dalle carezze si ritira,
>   Ma non morde, non graffia, o cozza, o tira?

Malatesti also treated it (*Sfinge*, I, no. 67), elaborating the theme into a sonnet. Catone l'Uticense, not satisfied with a sonnet to the snail (*Enimmi*, no. 68), also describes in another (no. 69) the slug. His version of the snail follows.

Quando che mi conviene uscir di casa,
    Di dietro esco, e d'avanti a un tempo stesso:
    E a quel che fo la gente è persuasa
    Ch'esca fuori di me, qual matta, spesso.

Perchè molto ho timor d'esser invasa,
    Sopra del dorso un moriglion mi ho messo.
    Se tengo poi la testa ignuda e rasa,
    Scusin l'error de l'inesperto sesso.

Armata ancora vò di doppia smarra;
    Ma ad ogni incontro in fodro la ripongo;
    Piacendomi così far la bizarra.

Stommi in casa racchiusa un tempo longo,
    E 'l mio stomaco assai sputa, e scatarra:
    Da l'umido abitar venir suppongo.

Symphosius appears to have had a natural weakness for crawling animals, because in his riddles a place of honor is assigned to lice, which he describes thus:

Est nova nostrarum cunctis captura ferarum,
    Ut si quid capias, id tibi ferre recuses,
    Et quid non capias, tecum tamen ipse reportes.[95]

According to an ancient tradition, the failure to guess the meaning of this description proved fatal to Homer and led him, not too prematurely, to his grave. Less fatal but equally annoying versions of lice may be found in other tongues. Italian riddles present a few. Croce (*Notte sollazzevole*, I, no. 51, p. 285) describes the birth and habitat of the louse, emphasizes its car-

---

[95] Ohl, p. 30.

nivorous and sanguivorous nature, and tells us that, eventually, ten brothers (human fingers) seize it and kill it:

> Di carne humana in questo mondo nasco,
>   e me ne vivo in selva folta, e scura,
>   e sol di carne mi nutrisco, e pasco,
>   e bevo il sangue in vece d'acqua pura;
>   ma perchè spesso simil cibo intasco,
>   e perchè troppo torno à la pastura,
>   vengon dieci fratelli à l'espedita,
>   e fra due ossi mi toglion la vita.

A much less elaborate and quite conventional version, is this: "Qual è quella cosa che quando la ni piglia, la non si ha, e quando la non si piglia la si ha?"[96]

Many of Symphosius' riddles are rather sophisticated literary inventions. The allusion in

> Littera sum caeli penna perscripta volanti,
> Bella cruenta gerens volucri discrimine Martis;
> Nec vereor pugnas, dum non sit longior hostis[97]

is so difficult that we may justifiably have recourse to Ohl's translation: "A letter of the sky am I, written with flying pen [or: wing],[98] waging bloody wars with Mars' swift hazard; nor do I fear fighting, provided that not taller be the foe." The letter referred to is the Upsilon or Lambda made in the sky by flying cranes, and the last line refers to the war of the cranes

---

[96] G. Rua, "Di alcune stampe d'indovinelli," *Archivio per lo studio delle tradizioni popolari*, VII (1888), 461. See De Filippis, p. 5.

[97] No. 26.

[98] A pun is intended.

and the pygmies. The author has clearly exceeded the limits of easy intelligibility. An ant riddle accumulates details without suggesting a contradiction:

> Provida sum vitae, duro non pigra labore,
> Ipsa ferens umeris securae praemia brumae.
> Nec gero magna simul, sed congero multa vicissim.[99]

Symphosius' description of a bookworm,

> Littera me pavit, nec quid sit littera novi,
> In literis vixi, nec sum studiosor inde.
> Exedi Musas, nec adhuc tamen ipsa profeci,[100]

is perhaps worthy of mention as the first of a long line of riddles on the theme.[101]

Symphosius is the acknowledged model of a very important school of riddlers who flourished in England in the seventh and eighth centuries and extended their influence to vernacular riddles in England and, through Anglo-Saxon missionaries, to Latin riddlemasters on the continent of Europe. I shall mention here only the Latin riddles and take up the vernacular riddles later.

After Symphosius, the first Latin riddler is the anonymous author of the so-called Berne Riddles, a collection of sixty-two "hexasticha rhythmica barbarie horride" written at Bobbio in the seventh century.[102] One manuscript contains an additional riddle

---

[99] No. 22.
[100] No. 16.
[101] See p. 94 below.
[102] For references see Tupper, *The Riddles of the Exeter Book*, pp. xlvi-xlvii; Max Manitius, *Geschichte der lateinischen Literatur im Mittelalter* (Munich, 1911 et seqq.), I, 192–193; II, 798.

that may not have belonged to the original collection. In the Middle Ages these riddles circulated under the name of Tullius. They have been printed half a dozen times in the nineteenth century. Manitius goes so far as to call the author an Irish monk, but there is no support for so definite an identification. The subjects of the riddles are folk themes: abstractions are avoided, and there is only one reference each to Eve, classical mythology, and history. Although ten themes are shared with Symphosius, there is no evidence of direct borrowing. Nevertheless, Tupper correctly says, "No doubt . . . the Berne enigmas belong to the same circle of thought as the Anglo-Latin problems; and, although no English manuscript of them exists, we are not surprised to find them followed by riddles of Aldhelm in Paris MS. 5596." The Berne Riddles are especially interesting for the author's familiarity with the North Italian landscape and its plants. Whoever he was, we may safely call him the first medieval riddle-master in Italy. A fair illustration of his style is a parallel to Jehuda Halevi's New Hebrew riddle for wheat:

> Mortem ego pater libens adsumo pro natis
> et tormenta simul, cara ne pignora tristem.
> Mortuum me cuncti gaudent habere parentes,
> et sepultum nullus parvo vel funere plangit.
> Vili subterrena pusillus tumulor urna,
> sed maiore possum post mortem surgere forma.[103]

---

[103] Berne Riddles, no. 12. See De Filippis, pp. 22–23, 76, 85, 109–114. The relations of riddles on this theme repay study.

The Englishman Aldhelm (d. 709), who is supposed
to have written his collection of one hundred riddles
between 685 and 705, is the most important figure in
the school of Anglo-Latin riddlemasters.[104] He drew
freely on Symphosius and may have known the Berne
collection. He showed considerable independence in
using his models, and added many new themes. His
riddles are especially important to the student of cul-
tural and technological history, for they preserve details of Old English life that cannot easily be found
elsewhere. For example, his description of the cucuma
duplex or authepsa (no. 54), a double cooking vessel
that held both fire and water, somewhat like a samo-
var, shows that eighth-century Englishmen knew an
achievement of Roman technology that Cicero had
praised and that Heliogabalus had somewhat imprac-
tically caused to be made in silver. His version of the
silkworm (no. 12), which is really a moth caterpillar
confused by Aldhelm with the silkworm, may be
quoted here because the same theme was to reappear
frequently in Italy and elsewhere[105] in the sixteenth
and later centuries:

> Annua dum redeunt texendi tempora telas,
> Lurida setigeris reduntant viscera filis,

---

[104] Tupper, *Exeter Book*, pp. xxxi–xxxiii; Manitius, I, 136–138. See also
the translation by John H. Pitman, *The Riddles of Aldhelm* ("Yale
Studies in English," LXVII, New Haven, 1925), and the valuable discussion of technological details in Erika von Erhardt-Siebold, *Die lateinischen Rätsel der Angelsachsen* ("Anglistische Forschungen," LXI,
Heidelberg, 1925). This deals not only with Aldhelm, but also with all
the other Old English writers of Latin riddles.

[105] See De Filippis, pp. 19–22, 68, 81.

> Moxque genestarum frondosa cacumina scando,
> Ut globulos fabricans tum fati sorte quiescam.

Interesting because of the favor it found in Europe in later centuries is his treatment of salt:

> Dudum limpha fui squamoso pisce redundans,
> Sed natura novo fati discrimine cessit,
> Torrida dum calidos patior tormenta per ignes:
> Nam cineri facies nivibusque simillima nitet.[106]

Other themes treated by Aldhelm which will find special favor later are the earth (no. 1), wind (no. 2), moon (no. 6), file (no. 21), cock (no. 26), water (no. 29), fire (no. 44), candle (no. 52), pen (no. 59), unicorn (no. 60), sword (no. 61), sieve (no. 67), trumpet (no. 68), sun and moon (no. 79), basilisk (no. 88), and night (no. 97). His version of the sword is worth quoting:

> De terrae gremiis formabar primitus arte;
> Materia trucibus processit cetera tauris
> Aut potius putidis constat fabricata capellis.
> Per me multorum clauduntur lumina leto,
> Qui domini nudus nitor defendere vitam.
> Nam domus est constructa mihi de tergore secto
> Necnon et tabulis, quas findunt stipite, rasis.[107]

Angiolo Cenni, Straparola, Ascanio de Mori, Stigliani, and several other Italian riddlers later treated, somewhat independently, most of these themes.

Archbishop Tatwine of Canterbury, who died in

---

[106] No. 19. See De Filippis, pp. 47, 64–65, 85, 97–98.
[107] See De Filippis, pp. 11–12, 93–95.

734, wrote forty riddles, one-third of them on religious or churchly themes.[108] The ingenuity with which he constructed them appears in the introductory couplet:

> Sub deno quater haec diverse enigmata torquens
> Stamine metrorum exstructor conserta retexit.

The first line of this couplet contains the initial letters of the forty riddles, and the second line contains, in reverse order, the initial letters of the last word in the first lines. We can therefore be certain that Tatwine wrote only forty riddles and that they are preserved to us in the order in which he arranged them. His choice of such subjects as philosophy, the four ways of interpreting a text, and the prepositions that govern two cases shows his love for abstractions. The riddle for the eyes shows his elaboration of the folk comparison to twins separated by a hill:

> Discernens totum juris natura locavit
> Nos pariter geminos una de matre creatos;
> Divisi haud magno parvi discrimine collis,
> Ut numquam vidi illum, nec me viderat ipse,
> Sed cernit sine me nihil, illo nec sine cerno.

Tatwine occasionally borrows phrases from Aldhelm, but he avoids using the same subjects.

Eusebius, who has been tentatively identified with Hwætberht, abbot of Wearmouth in Northumbria, wrote sixty riddles to complete the century begun by Tatwine.[109] The themes begin with God, an angel,

---

[108] Tupper, *The Riddles of the Exeter Book*, pp. xxxii–xxxiv; Manitius, I, 204–206.

[109] Tupper, *Exeter Book*, pp. xxxiv–xxxvi; Manitius, I, 206–207.

man, the sky, and the letters of the alphabet. The last
of these will illustrate the author's style:

> Innumere sumus et simul omnes queque sonamus,
> Una loqui nequit; nos tetre ludimus albis;
> Et licet alta loquamur, non sonus auribus instat;
> Preteritum loquimur, presens et multa futura.

He concludes with a score of zoölogical riddles based
on information found in the handbooks of Solinus and
Isidor. Such themes as the dragon, tiger, panther,
chameleon, leopard, scorpion, chimera, and ostrich
are obviously suited only to learned elaboration and
have no background in folk riddles. We can dispense
with an example of these artificial constructions.

The great missionary bishop, Boniface, who lived
from about 680 to 754 and was therefore a contemporary of Aldhelm, Tatwine, and Eusebius, chose ten
virtues and ten vices as the themes of his riddles.[110] In
an introduction of twenty hexameters dedicating
them to the abbess of Bischofsheim he compares the
virtues to the golden apples of the tree of life, and the
vices to the bitter fruit of the tree of which Adam ate.
His highly sophisticated manner appears further in
the acrostic formed by the initial letters of each riddle.
The acrostic gives the answer. Not content with this
complication, Boniface introduced into his first riddle
a second acrostic on the abbess' name. I choose the
briefest of these awkward and difficult allegories as
an illustration.

---

[110] Tupper, *Exeter Book*, pp. xliv–xlv; Manitius, I, 150–151.

[Spes Fatur]

S ancta comes faustus omnes comitata perhortor
P erpetuam meritis caelo comprendere vitam.
E t sine me scandit nullus per culmina caeli,
S ed tristem ac miseram post illinc facta secernunt:
F ortunata nimis, si non mentita fuissem,
A urea promittens starent ut ludicra mundi.
T errigenas jugiter duco ad caelestia regna,
V iribus ut freti tradant ad corpora poenas,
R egmina venturi captantes aurea saecli.

The so-called Lorsch riddles[111]—twelve in number—are found in a ninth-century Vatican manuscript from the Rhenish monastery of Lorsch. Their English origin or inspiration is generally conceded, for they appear in conjunction with the riddles of Aldhelm and Symphosius and show similarities in themes and phraseology to the riddles of Aldhelm, Tatwine, and Eusebius. Although the themes are those used in folk riddles (we might perhaps except the first two riddles with the answers "man" and "heart," which do not have many folk parallels), the treatment and the details chosen by the poet for elaboration have little in common with folk versions. The description of snow is as follows:

Nubibus e tetris vidi dilabere quandam:
Ipsa velox cecedit super ardua tecta domorum,
Mollis erat visu nec non lenissima tactu.

---

[111] See Tupper, *Exeter Book*, pp. xlvii–xlviii. Manitius gives them only ten lines in a footnote; see I, 151, n. 2. I have quoted nos. 6, 8, and 9 from Ernest Dümmler, *Poetae latini aevi Carolini*, I (Berlin, 1881), 20–23.

> Inde cadens iosumque cavavit leniter asprum
> Dura super terram, sibimet quae terga cadenti
> Praebuit, infixus terrae stabilisque manendo.[112]

This is quite different from the old and very popular comparison of snow to a white bird that flies without wings. An egg is a favorite theme of folk riddlers, but they do not use the details found in

> En video sobolem propria cum matre morantem,
> Mandre cuius pellis in pariete pendet adhaerens.

The folk theme of sowing seeds in the riddle for writing appears in a very different form in

> Candida virgo suas lacrimas dum seminat atras,
> Tetra per albentes linquit vestigia campos,
> Lucida stelligeri ducentia ad atria caeli.

This last riddle is especially interesting for the reminiscences of Tatwine, Aldhelm, and Eusebius pointed out by Dümmler.

The riddles circulated in the Middle Ages under Bede's name consist of a collection of prose questions and answers on Biblical themes, an anthology of miscellaneous texts by Symphosius, Aldhelm, and unnamed authors, and the *Propositiones ad acuendos juvenes.*[113] The prose queries, which form but one of many medieval lists of such brain teasers, show no literary elaboration and need no further mention here. The anthology, to which Tupper gives the title of *Jocoseria*, is part of the Cambridge manuscript Gg.

---

[112] *Iosumque* is *deorsumque.*
[113] Tupper, *Exeter Book*, pp. xlvii–li.

V. 35, containing Symphosius and all the Anglo-Latin riddlemasters. The texts have little interest, but the very curious interlineal commentary shows how medieval men interpreted riddles. A similar commentary occurs in the recently discovered collection by Claretus that is mentioned below. The *Propositiones*, which belong to Alcuin and not to Bede, are arithmetical puzzles. The last Anglo-Latin collection, the *Versus cuiusdam Scotti de alfabeto*,[114] contains riddles on the letters of the alphabet. Although such riddles occur in Oriental collections and have often been the objects of versifications, I have not included them in this essay.

The influence of Symphosius which we have seen in Italy, in the Berne Riddles of the seventh century, and in England in the Anglo-Latin school of the seventh and eighth centuries, continues in the Belgian *Fecunda ratis*, written after 979 by Egbert of Liége,[115] and the *Delicie cleri*, written between 1054 and 1056 by a monk named Arnulf.[116] In this didactic poem are three riddles dealing with these subjects: virginity and the bee; Adam and Enoch; and the flight of the cranes in the shape of the letter "L," that is to say, Lambda. The last we recognize as one quoted above from Symphosius.

A difficult liturgical riddle in a pontifical of Nevers (1013–1065) will serve as an example of medieval

[114] Tupper, *Exeter Book*, pp. l–li; Manitius, I, 497, n. 1, and II, 806.
[115] Manitius, II, 537.
[116] Manitius, II, 588. The riddles are quoted on pp. 589–590.

enigmatic inventions. Since the text is not easily found, it is printed here with a translation generously supplied by my friend and colleague, E. H. Kantorowicz. It is as follows:

> Dupla materia formam mea sumit usia,
> Bannitis binis elementis onoma quinis,
> Contra naturam variam sortita figuram.
> Nam dum vivabam dicendi sorte cerebam;
> Et modo post mortem dicendi prefero sortem.
> Presul Hugo magnus, quem pontificaverat agnus,
> Post duplex esse me simplex duxit ad esse,
> Et sancto Cyrico voto concessit amico,
> Ut sanctus Cyricus merito sibi factus amicus,
> Esse quod est uine quo qui nil dicitur esse
> Post praesens esse placatum prebeat esse.

❖ ❖ ❖

My being is composed of a twofold material;
If the twofold elements are set aside, my name is fivefold;
Against its nature it has received a different form.
For, while I was alive, I had not the gift of speech;
And only after my death I achieved the gift of speech.
Bishop Hugo the Great, whom the lamb made a pontiff,
Has reduced me—after my double existence—to simple
    existence,
And has conceded me by a vow to St. Cyr, his friend,
That St. Cyr may truly become his friend,
So that the being without whose being nothing can be
    called being
May grant him after the present a pacified being.[117]

---

[117] See Bibliothèque nationale, MS lat. 17333, fol. 18; A.-J. Crosnier (ed.), *Sacramentarium ad usum Aecclesiae Nivernensis* (Nevers, 1873); also *Dictionnaire d' archéologie et de liturgie chrétienne*, XII, 1, col. 1157.

The answer is, a book, which describes itself as made of two elements, ink and parchment, or, perhaps, the two syllables *li-ber*. If we disregard this dual aspect, the name is fivefold, being composed of five letters. Contrary to its nature, the parchment has been transfigured by the letters of the alphabet through which it now speaks. Such subtleties are often found in Byzantine riddling.

An interesting collection of more than a hundred and fifty late medieval riddles has only recently been discovered. It was made by a fourteenth-century Bohemian writer, who identifies himself in an acrostic as Doctor Claretus.[118] Although he knew some riddles belonging to the long literary tradition that we have been discussing, he draws chiefly on oral tradition for his materials. The riddles are introduced by a framework story of the sort previously described: a clever girl answers a wise man's questions and then asks some that he cannot answer. This story is, however, quickly dropped.

The year riddle that we have already found in the Orient occurs in Doctor Claretus in the following form:

> Una means arbos retinet ramos duodenos,
> omnis enim rami restant nisi bis duo nidi,
> quolibet in nido septem volucres retinendo.
> Quevis ibi volucrum recipit nomen propriatum;
> gignere non cessat cum mundo vivere restat.[119]

---

[118] Voclav Flajšhans, *Klaret a jeho družina*, Sbirka pramenů, skupina I, řada I, corpus I, i and ii (Prague, 1926–1928). For the acrostic see Bohumil Ryba, in *Listy filologické*, LXIV (1937), 266–267.

[119] For comments on this riddle see Wesselski, p. 375. For the text see Claretus, p. 66, and compare p. 73, no. 95.

More interesting than the year riddle is a curious description of five brothers who are interpreted as either the five senses or the five leaves beneath a rose blossom. Claretus, who seems to have intended the former answer (although a glossator wrote in words referring to a rose), has the girl put her opponent into confusion with

> Sunt quini fratres, bini barbaque carentes
> et duo barbati; quintum generis probo neutri.[120]

The eyes and ears might be called bearded or hairy, the tongue and the fingers lack hair, and the nose can perhaps be termed *generis neutri*. Most of us will probably find it easy to understand why a learned man could not guess the answer. The much older Berne Riddles preserve a trace of this invention:

> Pulchra in angusto me mater concipit alvo
> Et hirsuta barbis quinque conplectitur ulnis.
> Quae licet parentum parvo sim genere sumpta,
> Honor quoque mihi concessus fertur ubique.
> Utero cum nascor, matri rependo decorem
> Et parturienti nullum infligo dolorem.[121]

Among the various Renaissance versions, an English text in the Holme Riddles of the mid-seventeenth century will be a sufficient illustration: "There is a thing which hath five chins. Two hath beards, two hath none, and one it hath but half an one.—A rose bud whose outward green leaves are some jagged,

---

[120] See Wesselski, p. 373.
[121] Berne Riddles, no. 34. For editions see the Bibliography.

other plain."[122] This riddle, which comes ultimately from India, is an instructive example of the learned transmission of themes over long periods of time and wide stretches of country.

As in the cock riddle (no. 2), Claretus often included the answers in his verses:

> Ruffus cum barba visus cantare propheta,
> Qui bis erat natus et ter baptismata nactus,
> Huic usus digne pro nobis: gallus in igne.

In a few of Claretus' riddles some interlinear glosses give a strange interpretation in religious terms. Thus, in "Alat alis, quamvis caret alis: nix michi solvis" (no. 14), "volat ad celum" is written above the first two words and "anima" above "nix." In "Hospes ab ore tacet, loquitur domus: est aqua, pisces" (no. 27), "Christus" stands above the first and "ecclesia" above the last word. This riddle is immediately followed by the famous comparison of catching fish to capturing a house and its occupants. The editor has not separated them in his numbering, although the presence of the answer in the line here quoted, as well as the variants in oral tradition, indicates that we are dealing with two distinct riddles. The glossator soon ceases to give religious interpretations.

The riddles versified by Doctor Claretus usually consist of a single line and are almost entirely from folk sources. For example, the riddle (no. 110) comparing smoke to a son born before his father is known almost everywhere:

---

[122] Tupper, "Holme Riddles," no. 144. I have modernized the orthography.

> Filius est captus super edem, quam pater ortus:
> Ante salit fumus supra, quam fit bonus ignis.

The year riddle occurs a second time in a version (no. 95) resembling many Slavic folk texts:

> Sunt sexaginta volucres cum quinque trecente
> Atque duodeni griffones tres quoque nidi,
> Hii simulac unum generant ovumque per annum:
> Annus habendo dies numero festivaque menses.

"Abs pede currit aqua, globus et rota, viva metalla" (no. 97), with its various answers, is a folk riddle. An analogue to the English cherry riddle of Dick Redcap appears in "Saxosum corpus rubeam tunicam tenet unus" (no. 76).

The far from classical verses of Doctor Claretus did not circulate widely. Only two manuscripts have been discovered. On reading them, one often agrees with the author's introductory remark, "Enigma est sermo difficilis et miraculosus." Although their literary worth is slight, their value as early versions of many folk themes has not yet been fully exploited.

The riddles of Johann Hauser (*ca.* 1440–1518), a Benedictine monk at Mondsee in Upper Austria and later a secular priest, still lie unpublished in manuscripts at Vienna.[123] Hauser was a collector of Latin and German poems, a translator, a lexicographer, and a writer of verse. In a retrospective glance at his own life that he wrote on his fiftieth birthday, he said that

---

[123] See Hermann Menhardt in *Verfasserlexikon des deutschen Mittelalters*, II (Berlin, 1936), cols. 227–228.

he had always postponed original composition and now it had become too difficult for him. His bent was didactic, as appears from his translation of the Bible, a Latin index to the Bible, and his *Pharetra doctorum* (1485), an alphabetical subject index to the Church Fathers.

Another late medieval riddlemaster is, unfortunately, known only by name. Johannes Noblet, a French Carmelite who lived about 1430, wrote a *Centiloquium aenigmatum*, but his work, which continues the old tradition of a century of riddles, seems to have been lost.[124]

After 1500 a new interest in literary riddles appears in Renaissance and Reformation Germany. The casual writing of riddles as a variety of epigram gave way to a livelier interest. Italian scholars discussed the history of riddling and gave space to it in their handbooks of poetics. A few pedants wrote Latin riddles, and many poetasters composed them in Italian. In Germany the situation was almost precisely the opposite in every particular. Although many wrote Latin riddles, the handbooks of poetics scarcely mention the subject. Many scholars wrote Latin riddles, but before the seventeenth century virtually no one except the early Meistersinger, who concealed their inventions in the closed circle of their schools, wrote

---

[124] See Johann Albert Fabricius, *Bibliotheca mediae et infimae latinitatis*, III (Florence, 1858), 394. He is repeating the information in Johannes Tritheim, *De scriptoribus ecclesiaticis* (1494). J. G. Schelhorn rejects the suggestion that Noblet had discovered the century of riddles written by Symphosius; see *Amoenitates litterariae* (Frankfurt a. M., 1725), II, 473–475.

German riddles. Other countries showed little interest in riddles, either in Latin or in the vernacular, before 1600. Folk riddles and tricky questions, which no doubt circulated as widely then as now, were printed in France[125] not long before 1500 and in Germany a little later.[126] Although printers apparently found such collections profitable ventures, literary riddling does not seem to draw heavily on them.

One of the first signs of a revival of interest in riddling was a treatise by the Italian humanist Lilio Gregorio Giraldi (1479–1552). In his *Aenigmatum ex antiquis scriptoribus collectorum libellus singularis* he compiled everything he could find on the subject in the Latin and Greek classics. After its first appearance in 1551, the book was several times reprinted.[127] He apparently thought it a contribution to classical studies, for he made no reference to the growing contemporary interest in vernacular riddling. For more than three centuries Giraldi's little book has remained the best account of classical riddling, and it is still the most convenient place in which to find these materials.

---

[125] *Les Adeuineaux amoureux* (see the *Gesamtkatalog der Wiegendrucke*, I, Leipzig, 1925, nos. 222, 223). See a reprint, in eighty-six copies, in the series "Joyeusetés facéties," VI (Paris, Techener, 1831).

[126] *Strassburger Räthselbuch* (*ca.* 1505), reprinted by A. F. Butsch (Strassburg, 1876). See the excerpts from a related Augsburg chapbook of about 1515 in Wilhelm Wackernagel, *Zeitschrift für deutsches Altertum*, III (1843), 25–34.

[127] I have not seen the original edition (Basel, 1551), nor the reprint in Giraldi, *Opera* (Basel, 1580), II, 446 ff. I have used the reprint in Nicolaus Reusner, *Aenigmatographia* (Frankfurt a. M., 1602). This does not differ from the 1599 edition, which I have compared.

Giraldi's treatise did not inspire Italians to write Latin riddles. A brief mention in Julius Caesar Scaliger's *Poetices* (1561) refers to them as a genre allied to the epigram and cites Athenaeus as an authority.[128] Although Scaliger had little to say in his treatise, he composed more Latin riddles than any other Italian writer. "Plurima fecimus nos," as he modestly says.[129] His style is wholly literary and shows only the scantest traces of folk influence. He has a few riddles on abstract themes such as God, necessity, nature, fate, and hope. A short one on luck (*casus*) will illustrate them:

> Quod tibi nec fortuna dabit, nec fata dedere,
>   Hoc ero: sed quod sim, forte scio nec ego.[130]

Although most of Scaliger's themes appear also in folk riddles, his treatment is quite different. His riddles contain no passages deserving the condemnation which Gilles Ménage uttered regarding his epigrams.[131] His comparison of day and night to sister and brother might be a folk theme:

> Quale animal, dic, esse putes, quod nobile totum.
>   Est oculus, neque pars praeterea ulla manet?
> Quotidie gignit natum sine matre creatum
>   Qui tamen una ipsa hac interit ille die.
> Cuius item soror absente est genitore creata,
>   Partita imperium fratris, et interitum.[132]

---

[128] See *Poetices*, I (ed. Heidelberg, 1617, pp. 122–123), cap. 57. See also III, cap. 83 (p. 319).

[129] See Reusner, *Aenigmatographia*, pp. 165–203. The riddles were printed in his *Poemata*; see the edition without place of 1591, I, 546 ff.

[130] Reusner, p. 167.

[131] *Ménagiana*, IV, 96.

[132] Reusner, pp. 167–168.

His mirror riddle is, for example, quite different from
the popular treatment of the subject:

> Mira tibi mater rerum foecunda novarum,
>   Quin etiam tecum tibi saepe parit.
> Foetus tam similis tibi, ne magis esse potis sit,
>   Attamen illius dextra sinistra tua est.[133]

In his description of a riddle, he expects the hearer to
know that the ancient Greeks rewarded him who suc-
ceeded in guessing a riddle, and condemned him who
failed to drink wine mixed with sea water. Such
knowledge cannot properly be required in a riddle:

> Quaenam sunt tenebrae placidi tegumenta laboris,
>   Sub quibus urbani lux latet alma salis?
> Mos fuit antiquis, victori dona corollas,
>   Sed victo muriae pocula plena dare.
> Non ea barbaries nostras nunc asperat umbras,
>   Sat poena, et praemi risus utrinque levis.[134]

Scaliger's literary exercises are better than many
similar efforts written in the next three centuries, but
the world has passed them by without great loss.

Among the few Latin riddles written in Italy at this
time, Angelo Poliziano's enigmatic epitaph has a place
of unique interest and importance. His verses

> Hoc est sepulchrum, intus cadaver non habens,
> Hoc est cadaver, est sepulchrum non habens,
> Sed est idem cadaver, est sepulchrum idem

---

[133] Reusner, p. 177. This theme is discussed in greater detail by De
Filippis, pp. 114–119.
[134] Reusner, p. 203.

are a rewriting of an epigram in the Greek Anthology.[135] This epigram was perhaps also known to him in a version by Ausonius. Poliziano supposed it an epitaph for Niobe, but a commentator on Genesis and others have thought that it suited Lot's wife.[136] Even as late as the mid-eighteenth century, attempts were made at naming the person intended.[137] As an example of this persistent interest in the epitaph we may note the following eighteenth-century verses from a manuscript in the British Museum:

> Stay, Traveler, and wondering here behold
> A Tomb, which doth within no corps enfold.
> Said I, a Tomb? Here I mistaken was,
> It is a Corps and wants a Tomb, alas!
> Was I mistaken? No, for it is either;
> Nay, it is both, and truly it is neither.[138]

A still more interesting use of the Greek epigram is seen in the last lines of what is purported to be an ancient inscription. During the Renaissance, this inscription was preserved at Bologna in a version which lacked the epigram, and at Milan in another version which ended with the epigram. Renaissance scholars

---

[135] See the editions of Brunck or Jacobs, no. 613, and VII, 311, in modern editions; Ausonius, *Epitaphia*, 29; Poliziano in Reusner, *Aenigmatographia*, ed. 1602, p. 307, and Friedreich, p. 208. For adaptations by Italian authors see Hutton, p. 494. The wording of the last line often varies.

[136] The commentator is Cornelius a Lapide; see *Notes and Queries*, 4th Series, VIII (1871), 92.

[137] *Royal Magazine*, V (1761), 44, as cited in *Notes and Queries*, 4th Series, VIII (1871), 56.

[138] Tupper, "Holme Riddles," note on no. 11, quoting MS Harl. 7316, p. 58.

heatedly discussed the relations of the two versions, sought to prove or disprove their authenticity, and struggled vainly to interpret them. They proposed, it has been said, at least forty different solutions.[139] Probably no riddle has attracted more scholarly attention, and certainly none has so successfully kept its secret. Even in the nineteenth century, Sir Walter Scott could mention it as a theme worthy of the zeal of that worthy antiquary Jonathan Oldbuck.[140]

The following version with the title "Aenigma Bononiense" is actually the text in the Milanese manuscript:

Aelia Lelia Crispis
Nec vir nec mulier nec Androgyna
Nec puella nec iuvenis nec anus
Nec casta nec meretrix nec pudica
Sed omnia
Sublata nec fame nec veneno
Sed omnibus
Nec cælo nec aquis nec terris
Sed ubique iacet

[139] See James Crossley, *Notes and Queries*, 1st Series, III (1851), 338–339. He apparently planned a treatise on the epitaph, but I have not found that he printed anything more than this note. A few titles will show how great an interest the epitaph aroused in our period: Richard White of Basingstoke, *Aelia Laelia Crispis, Epitaphium Antiquum quod in Agro Bononiensi adhuc videtur, a diversis interpretatum varie, novissime autem . . . explicatum* (Padua, 1568); Ioa. Turrius, *Epistola super Aenigmate Aelia Laelia Crispis* (Dordrecht, 1618); Fort. Licetus, *Ad Aelia Laelia Crispis Aristotelicum Aenigma Allegoriae peripateticae de generatione et provatione Libri II* (Venice, 1629; Padua, 1630); Y. C. C. Malvasia, *Aelia Laelia Crispis non nata resurgens in expositione legali* (Bologna, 1683). The first three are cited from Martin Lipenius, *Bibliotheca philosophica* (Frankfurt a. M., 1682), I, 14. The last is in the Fontana Library of the University of California, Berkeley.

[140] *The Antiquary*, chap. xiv.

Lelia Crispis alia in cavo acuto
Lucius Agatho Priscius
Nec maritus nec amator nec necessarius
Neque moerens neque gaudens neque flens
Hanc nec molem nec pyramidem nec sepulcrum
Sed omnia
Scit et nescit quid cui posuerit
Hoc est sepulcrum intus cadaver non habens
Hoc est cadaver sepulcrum extra non habens
Sed cadaver idem est & sepulcrum sibi.[141]

The identification of Aelia Laelia Crispis remains wholly obscure. Some have found her to be the soul, a eunuch, the water of the sky, Niobe, quicksilver, and even Pope Joan. We shall not disturb her quiet by asking troublesome questions.

The memorial to Aelia Laelia Crispis inspired an entirely apocryphal epitaph of Andrew Turnecoate (Andreas Vortunius, as the original inventor of the figure named him). In John Healey's *Discovery of a New World, or a Description of the South Indies, hitherto unknown, by an English Mercury*, which is a free translation or paraphrase of Bishop Joseph Hall's *Mundus alter et idem*,[142] we read the following epitaph:

Stay, reade, walke, Here lieth Andrew Turnecoate, who was neither Slave, nor Soldier, nor Phisitian, nor Fencer, nor Cobbler, nor Filtcher, nor Lawier, nor Usurer, but all;

---

[141] Malvasia, *op. cit.*, p. 23. Malvasia gives a detailed account of the variant readings.

[142] See *Notes and Queries*, 1st Series, III (1851), 242, 339 (not 329, as in the Index). Hall's *Mundus alter et idem* was printed without date [1605] at Frankfurt a. M., and reprinted at Hanau in 1607 and at Utrecht in 1643. John Healey's *Discovery* was printed about 1609.

who lived neither in citty, nor countrie, nor at home, nor abroade, nor at sea, nor at land, nor here, nor elsewhere, but everywhere. Who died neither of hunger, nor poyson, nor hatchet, nor halter, nor dogge, nor disease, but altogether. I, I. H. . . , being neither his debtour, nor heire, nor kinsman, nor friend, nor neighbour, but all: in his memory have erected this, neither monument, nor tombe, nor sepulchre, but all: wishing neither evill nor well, neither to thee, nor to mee, nor him, but all unto all.

For reasons which are quite obscure, Protestant German scholars, especially those resident in western Germany, showed a great liking for riddles. Although such humanists as the Bohemian Bohuslaus Felix Lobkovitz (d. 1510) and the Erfurt reformer Helius Eobanus Hessus (1488–1540) wrote them, their verses are comparable to the casual scribblings of their Italian contemporaries. Reusner's *Aenigmatographia* makes it easy to survey such by-products of the poetic muse. We shall comment here only on those writers who issued separate books of riddles. They were, as we have said, almost exclusively Protestants who lived in western Germany or who removed to that region.

The first is Johannes Lorichius Secundus, of Hadamer. Although Goedeke ascribes[143] to him an *Aenigmatum libri tres* of 1528, the date must be an error. It cannot be reconciled with his enlistment in the army after the siege of Frankfurt in 1552, his subsequent

---

[143] *Grundriss*, II, 92, sec. 113, no. 20. See also J. G. Schelhorn, *Amoenitates litterariae* (Frankfurt, 1725), II, 482–483.

visit to a brother in Lithuania, and his later study of
law at Orleans which prepared him for his ten years
of service to William of Orange. He died in a skirmish
in 1569. The three books of riddles by Lorichius were
first printed at Marburg in 1540. The final edition[144] is
that of 1545. I have used Reusner's selections in the
Aenigmatographia.

Lorichius versified many folk riddles and often set
German originals beside his Latin texts. His arbutus
riddle is, for example, closely allied to the modern
English description of Dick Redcap or the cherry:

> Dic, quid multa sinu circumfert saxa tumenti,
>> Et socios inter cernitur usque suos.
> Purpureo ante alios laetum se jactat amictu:
>> Urbibus excessit, ruraque grata colit.
> Non est, quod metuas, nisi tu prior ipse lacessas:
>> Hoc facturo, instant multa pericla tibi.
>>> Es hat sein Busen voll Steine
>>> Wirdt gefunden selten alleine
>>> Hat ein rothes Röcklein an
>>> Thet manchem nichts   liess ers stahn[145]

His coffin riddle is an early record of a very popular
western European theme:

> Qui manibus compinget opus, non indiget illo,
> Quique emit, hoc uti non vult, quique utitur ipso,
> Ignorat, quamvis habeat, tu solve, quid hoc sit.[146]

An *Aenigmatum centuria* by Ludovicus Helmbold
(1532–1598) without date or place of publication has

---

[144] A copy in the Libraries of the University of Chicago.
[145] *Aenigmatographia*, ed. 1602, p. 281.
[146] *Aenigmatographia*, ed. 1602, p. 291.

attracted little attention.[147] Helmbold (1532–1598),
who was born at Mühlhausen in Thuringia, was associated for a time with Erfurt but returned to Mühlhausen as a teacher and minister. He wrote many
hymns, among them a cycle of forty on marriage, and
some violent attacks on the Jesuits. The first of his
hundred riddles—all but a dozen are distichs—is a
fair sample of Helmbold's pedestrian style and thought:

> Debeor a quovis cuique, et dum pluribus unus
> Me reddit, multo plus habeat inde mei.

He withholds the answers to his inventions, but tells
us in the dedicatory verses:

> Ex Physicis quaedam, quaedam moralibus hausta,
> Quaedam etiam cernes esse petita sacris.

The *Aenigmata*[148]—one hundred and twenty in
number—of Johannes Lauterbach (1531–1593) circulated in manuscript during the sixteenth century,
for Reusner made selections from them for his anthology of 1599. They did not appear in print until 1601,
and were republished, as a supplement to Reusner's
Aenigmatographia, in 1602. Lauterbach, a native of
Upper Lusatia, spent his life as a teacher in Heil-
bronn. His long riddles are sufficiently illustrated by
his conception of a shadow:

> Sum brevis in medio, capite ac in calce diei
> Longior, ut surgit sole caditve jubar.

---

[147] See Goedeke, *Grundriss*, II, 195–196, sec. 127, no. 100, who cites a monograph on Helmbold by W. Thilo.

[148] Goedeke, *Grundriss*, II, 102, sec. 113, no. 84.

Urgentes fugio, fugientes insequor, istas
 Me videt alternis quisque subire vices.
Defessos recreo gratas dum largior auras,
 Dumque fatigatis praebeo frigus humo.
Nil fraudes vereor, mala nil discrimina, meque
 Sede, prior moveat se nisi, nemo movet.

He chooses such learned themes as case (grammatical), Tiresias, Solomon, nobody (Nemo), anger, old age, and shows little familiarity with folk riddles in either form or matter.

Like Johannes Lauterbach, Nicolaus Reusner (1545–1602) went from eastern to western Germany to make his scholarly fortune.[149] He was much more successful than his predecessor, for he attained notable success and was, at the time of his death, rector magnificus of the University of Jena. Before he had reached the age of forty he had published (among other books) a *Hodoeporicum sive itinerarium totius fere orbis libri VII*, an essay on bathing resorts, and an important collection of biographies, as well as some Latin verse. His last scholarly work was a treatise on riddling combined with an anthology.[150] I mention him here for his *Aenigmata*, printed in the last year of his life. These artfully condense the matter of a riddle into a distich, but display more skill in rhetoric than poetic feeling. For the old riddle of day and night—which we have already found in the Rigveda—he wrote the following two lines.

---

[149] Goedeke, *Grundriss*, II, 109, sec. 113, no. 147.
[150] For comment on these see below, pp. 87–88.

> Sunt gemina germana, harum alteram et altera gignit,
>   Perque vices sic fit, filia nata, parens.[151]

His riddle for smoke is an echo of Symphosius:

> Lacryma multa mihi, sed nulla est causa doloris,
>   Coeli affecto vitam, sed gravis aer obest.[152]

Reusner's scholarly work on riddles did the cause better service than his verse.

The riddles of Johannes Pincier (d. 1624),[153] a doctor of medicine, who was born in the Wetterau in 1556 and was a student at Marburg and Heidelberg, were published at Herborn in 1605 and again at The Hague in 1665. Since they are later than the limits which I have set, I shall only note them as an instance of the western German tradition of riddling. I have not been able to discover when the first edition of Johannes Boemus, *Aenigmata sacra*, appeared. The second edition, which I have not seen, was printed in 1568. The book appears to belong to the same Protestant tradition. All or almost all of the collections which I have just described begin with riddles on sacred subjects and pass to questions about Biblical figures (arranged in rough chronological order) before giving riddles on miscellaneous themes.

Hadrian Junius (1511–1575), whom Gerard Johann Vossius singles out to praise as the most distinguished writer of Latin riddles in northern Europe, wrote an

---

[151] *Aenigmata*, p. 68.
[152] *Aenigmata*, p. 70.
[153] See Goedeke, *Grundriss*, II, 116, sec. 113, no. 227; *Allgemeine deutsche Biographie*, XXVI, 148–149.

Emblematum et aenigmatum libellus (1565), which Reusner included in his *Aenigmatographia*. There is, however, no evidence associating him with this company of Protestant German riddlers. The fact that Junius printed emblems with his riddles suggests another line of descent. Like Jacobus Masenius, S.J., whose *Speculum veritatis occultae* appeared two generations later,[154] Junius (who was a Protestant) was reflecting the Renaissance passion for emblematic and enigmatic concepts. This long line runs from Hierapollus Apollo to Colonna's *Hypnerotomachia* and the Egyptian speculations of that amazing Jesuit polyhistor, Athanasius Kircher.[155]

Junius, who wrote fifty riddles, often used folk themes. He versifies, for example, as a parallel to his first riddle for a pen the modern half-literary comparison to a thing which is not flesh and yet is torn from flesh, and labels it "e Gallico idiomate." The text is too long to quote. His equating of a hand to a tree is of folk origin:

> Porrigor in ramos quinos, et quilibet horum
> Diditur in triplices nodos, nisi quintus egeret
> Uno, qui solus respondet robore cunctis,
> Undique colliculis surgo, in vallemque resido,
> Ast abaci, desit si forte, ega munia praesto.[156]

His long riddle entitled *Synagraphum* (bond, treaty) has a parallel in the Renaissance and modern English

---

[154] Published at Cologne in 1650, it had a second edition in 1664.
[155] See his *Oedipus Aegyptiacus* (Rome, 1653), II, i, 27–36.
[156] No. 4.

> The calf, the goose, and the bee,
> The world is ruled by these three.
>> —Parchment, quill-pen and wax.

Junius's version

> Anser, apis, vitulis, rerum potiuntur, et orbis,
>> Tergeminum brutum frena superba regit,
> Res similis monstri, condigna inteprete, qualis
>> Thebigenae nodos solvere Sphingis amet,
> Membranam vitulus praebet, calamosque canorus
>> Anser, apes stipant cerea dona vagae,
> Fasque, nefasque tria haec obeunt, dum tergora chartae
>> Penna arat, obstringit cera notata fidem,
> Hic humana tribus divinaque jura reguntur,
>> Omneque momentum hoc cardine terna trahunt[157]

has a parallel in Sylvain's sonnet (no. 17):

> Trois, qui iamais ne furent d'un accord,
>> Grands biens & maux font paroistre en ce monde,
>> Dont le premier, qui de simplesse abonde
>> Pour cest effect, se laisse mettre à mort.

> Mesme au second on faict semblable tort,
>> Ou pour le moin rudement on le fonde,
>> Pour luy oster une chose assez ronde,
>> Laquelle estoit son ayde & son support.

> Le tiers perd parfois de son labeur
>> Ce que moins vaut, & laisse le meilleur,
>> Pour sustenter la creature humaine.

> Depuis long temps sont employez ainsi
>> Pour mettre au monde ennuy, peine, & soucy.
>> Qui sont ceux-cy qui ont, & donnent peine?

---

[157] No. 30.

The answer is given by the author himself, who writes: "Ces trois sont le Mouton, ou l'Agneau, l'Oye, & l'Abeille, par lesquels se faict bien & mal à cause des procés, car l'un produit le parchemin, que l'on faict de sa peau, l'autre les plumes pour escrire dessus, & l'Abeille produit la cire, où s'imprime le seel, & laisse le miel pour nourriture de l'homme."

Several contemporary treatises summarized and guided these Renaissance riddlers. We have already commented on Lilio Gregorio Giraldi's *Libellus*, an account of the art in classical times. A *Dialogus qui inscribitur enigma*[158] by Jacobus Pontanus, or Spanmüller (1542–1626), is only one of his many highly successful schoolbooks. Born at Brüx in Bohemia, Spanmüller was educated in Italy, where he adopted the name Pontanus. He became a member of the Society of Jesus and devoted his energies to writing textbooks and translating Greek. His textbooks were used widely for more than a century. His handbook of poetics (1594), which contains a chapter on the riddle, was, curiously enough, revised for use in Mexican schools in 1605 and thus shows how riddles were carried to the New World. The *Dialogus* exemplifies pleasantly the use of riddles in conversation, but does not contribute much to our knowledge of enigmatic style. Pontanus may have written some of the illustrative examples himself.

---

[158] I have used a reprint in Reusner, *Aenigmatographia* (1602). Seven of the riddles in the *Dialogus* may be found in the anonymous *Aenigmata et gryphi veterum ac recentium* (Douai, 1604). For a brief account of Pontanus see Hutton, pp. 65–66.

The riddler's encyclopedia is Nicolaus Reusner's *Aenigmatographia*.[159] This contains Giraldi's account of classical riddling, the *Dialogus* of Pontanus, the text of the allusions to riddles in classical authors, and excerpts from various Renaissance handbooks of poetics. In much the same way that the encyclopedias of Gronovius and Graevius summed up classical scholarship a century later, Reusner assembled all that there was to know about riddling. He neglected to mention some contemporary authors of Latin riddles, passed over texts in the vernacular, and showed no knowledge of folk riddles, but such omissions can scarcely be rated serious defects, and do not at all diminish the great merits of his work.

In addition to treatises on the art of riddling, scholars also made anthologies. By a curious coincidence three such books appeared in Germany in the same year, 1602. I have just mentioned the first and most important of them. It was Nicolaus Reusner's *Aenigmatographia*, which was a very large anthology as well as storehouse of learned discussion. Reusner reprinted the riddles of Symphosius and Aldhelm, a selection of Renaissance epigrammatists who had happened, like Thomas More and many another, to jot down an occasional riddle, and finally the works of the chief German enigmatographs of the sixteenth century. His duodecimo of 409 pages was issued

---

[159] Frankfurt a. M., 1599, 1602. The later edition adds much new matter. The existence of an edition of 1589 is almost certain, but no copy is known to exist. See J. G. Schelhorn, *Amoenitates literariae*, I (Frankfurt a. M., 1725), 477–480.

with three related works. These were the riddles
of Johannes Lauterbach, those of Nicolaus Reusner
himself, and the *Sylvula logogriphorum* (an anthology of charades and other manipulations of syllables
and letters); each had a separate title page, but the
pagination was continuous. An index to the four parts
united them. Although some Latin riddles written
before 1600 are lacking, Reusner made an amazingly
complete collection of permanent value.

A *Centuria prima selectissimorum juxta, et variae
jucunditatis aenigmatum*, by Johannes Fosterus (1576–
1613), has been inaccessible to me.[160] It may have
been a schoolbook or a collection of choice bits for the
general reader. Something of its character may perhaps be inferred from the life of Fosterus. He was
preacher at Leipzig, rector at Schneeberg, preacher at
Zeitz, professor at Wittenberg, and general superin-
tendent—a Lutheran dignitary something like a
bishop—at Mansfeld. His collection of riddles was published while he was a student of Lutheran theology
and rector of the school at Schneeberg. Johannes
Buchler's didactic purpose is clearly apparent in the
*Gnomologia seu sententiarum memorabilium, cum pri-
mis Germanicae linguae, brevis et aperta, Latino carmine,
inspersis rhythmis festivissimis, facta descriptio*,[161]
which first appeared in 1602. Although a Catholic,

---

[160] Cited from Karl Goedeke, *Grundriss zur Geschichte der deutschen
Dichtung*, 2d ed. (Dresden), II (1886), 115.
[161] The title here given is that of the third edition (Mainz, 1614).
Goedeke gives a different arrangement of words as the title of the first
edition; see *Grundriss*, II, 16, sec. 18.

Buchler, a teacher at Gladbach, was permitted to retain his position as a teacher. He wrote various textbooks and made several other collections of proverbs. Only in his *Gnomologia* did he include riddles, but here we can see his growing interest in them.[162] The second edition added a few new texts, and the third many more. Since the third edition has been generously placed at my disposal by Professor Richard Jente, of the University of North Carolina, I shall base my remarks on it.

It is difficult to discover Buchler's sources. In a chapter heading he says that he wrote some riddles and borrowed others. He tells us at times that he repeats Symphosius, but many Symphosian riddles appear without any notation. He credits some verses to Hadrian Junius, whom I have already mentioned. The well riddle,

> Dic quibus in terris et eris mihi magnus Apollo,
> Tres pateat coeli spatium non amplius ulnas,[163]

is properly recognized as Vergilian. Various questions belonging to the cycle of *L'Enfant sage* and its allied dialogues are quoted from Diogenes Laertius, with whose name they were associated at this time.

Clearly, Buchler was familiar with classical, medieval, and Renaissance riddling. He himself may be responsible for one or more of the versions of the

---

[162] Ed. 1602, pp. 326–373; ed. 1606, pp. 471–563 (pp. 100–199 are skipped in numbering); ed. 1614, pp. 402–499; ed. 1639, pp. 403–499.
[163] P. 455.

Sphinx riddle, which we may note as examples of variations possible in versifying a simple theme:

De Homine

Est animal totum per mundum non male notum,
    Mane quod it quadrupes, idque deinde bipes.
Ire tripes gaudet, cum mox sua tempora claudet.
    Quod sit si dicas alter Oedipus eas.
        Vel sic.
Quod pedibus binis animal meat absque ruinis,
    Claudicat hinc ternis, prorepsit et ante quaternis?
        Aliter.
Sphinx dedit aenigma hoc, quadrupes quae bestia
        quondam,
    Deinde bipes fieret, tandem eademque tripes.[164]

Buchler versifies many very curious folk riddles. He has the first recorded parallel to "It has a head like a cat, feet like a cat, a tail like a cat, but isn't a cat.—A kitten," which appears as

Quid lupi quaeso speciem rapacis
    Exprimis, formamque trucem, pilosque
Ut procul si tu videas, lupum ipsum
        Dixeris esse?
        Responsio.
Est lupa, quae similem formam sortita marito,[165]

and the modern "What grows smaller the more you add to it?—A hole," which is

Fit minus adijicias si quid; si demseris illi,
    Protinus augetur, dic quid id esse putes?[166]

---

[164] Pp. 448–449.
[165] P. 421.
[166] P. 447.

He gives perhaps the oldest version of the modern "What is it that you don't have and don't want, but if you had it, you wouldn't give it up for a thousand dollars?—One eye" as

> Non habeo, non habere velim, quod si tamen adsit,
> Non caream Croesi si mihi dentur opes.[167]

The Renaissance English fan or feather riddle,

> In open field I cannot lye,
> and yet may rest quietly
> within a box of ivory,[168]

has a parallel in his

> In campis aegre iaceo, atque patentibus arvis,
> Me bene conclusum scrinia parva tenent.[169]

His wide range of taste, which much exceeds that of the contemporary writers of riddles, appears in the inclusion of "Dic age cur piscis natat? alas adde volabit,"[170] which is akin to such statements of the obvious as "Why does a man cross the road?" His plays on letters and words resemble the previously quoted Sanskrit charade and the medieval liturgical riddle of Nevers. One example is sufficient:

> Ave, Salutem
> Mitto tibi navem prora, puppique carentem:
> Mitto tibi metulas, vertito si dubitas.[171]

---

[167] Ed. 3, p. 446.
[168] *A Booke of Merrie Riddles* (1631), no. 26 = Brandl, p. 56. Tupper, "Holme Riddles," p. 97, has the answer: fan.
[169] Ed. 3, p. 427.
[170] Ed. 3, p. 445.
[171] Ed. 3, p. 449.

Buchler prints two versions of the famous riddle for the fish in a net. The first reads as follows:

> Hospes cauponis quidam pervenit in aedes,
> > Nec cauponi hospes cognitus ante fuit:
> Per patulas domus hic elabitur ipsa fenestras,
> > Inque suo infelix hospite caupo manet.[172]

Only occasionally does he show off his learning, as in

> De vino aqua misto aenigma Rhythmicum

> In cratere meo Thetis est conjuncta Lyaeo,
> > Est Dea juncta Deo, sed Dea maior eo.
> Nil valet ipse Deus, Dea dum praesens manet ejus,
> > Detur propterea nunc Deus absque Dea.[173]

His most ambitious effort is perhaps the cock riddle. This contains traces of conceptions which we have already discussed and also some of Buchler's own invention:

> > Regium quidam diadema gestat
> > Miles, auratum gerit atque calcar,
> > Temporum vates, bonus et Propheta.
> > > Dic mihi quis sit?
> > Ipse materno teres, et rotundus
> > Ventre processit, nec habens caput, nec
> > Ceteros artus, animamque nullam.
> > > Dic rogo quis sit?
> > Inde natura melius favente,
> > Accipit sensus, animam, figuram,
> > Admonet caecos homines, docetque.
> > > Dic rogo quis est?

---

[172] Ed. 3, p. 419. See another version on p. 420.
[173] P. 445.

Prenditur, morte afficitur cruenta,
Veste nudatur per aquas calentes,
Ignibus tandem datur excoquendus.
        Dic rogo quis sit?[174]

An anonymous *Aenigmata et griphi veterum ac recentium*[175] was a Jesuit schoolbook. It is the first outward sign of the rising interest of that religious order in riddling. This book for use in French schools appeared half a century before the previously mentioned *Speculum veritatis occultae* of Jacobus Masenius, S.J. It is one of the few evidences of French interest in, or concern with, Latin riddling. It contrasts sharply with the great spurt in riddling in the vernacular which marks seventeenth- and eighteenth-century France. The *Aenigmata et griphi veterum ac recentium* contains a brief general introduction, seven riddles from the *Dialogus* by Jacobus Pontanus, a selection of Latin riddles, the century of Symphosius with the notes of Joseph Castalio, and a few riddles by Aldhelm and later writers.

The long line of Greek and Latin riddle writers inspired more or less directly the writing of riddles in the vernacular languages. Of course, Greek riddles are truly vernacular riddles. In western Europe the

---

[174] Pp. 430–431. I have corrected *roga* in the eighth line.

[175] Douai, 1604. A copy in the private library of Archer Taylor. See Brunet, *Manuel*, IV, 136. Two books which were published long after 1600 should be mentioned for their importance as anthologies. The *Oedipodiana seu Sphingis Aenigmata* appeared anonymously at Milan in 1720 and, under the name of its author, Franciscus a S. Barbara, at Oppau in 1732. The latter edition is greatly enlarged. Wilhelm Binder's *Flores aenigmatum latinorum* (Stuttgart, 1857) is an anthology of 400 riddles.

first literary riddles in a vernacular language are the Old English riddles of the *Exeter Book*. These are usually dated in the eighth century. Although they were suggested in part by Symphosius and his Anglo-Latin imitators and followers, the author shows much originality. Tupper and others have justly praised the vigorous conception and the poetic style of these riddles. The book-moth riddle[176] is supposed to be an imitation of the previously quoted riddles by Symphosius.[177] It is as follows:

> A moth ate a word! To me that seemed
> A strange thing to happen, when I heard that wonder,—
> A worm that would swallow the speech of a man.
> Sayings of strength steal, in the dark,
> Thoughts of the mighty; yet the thieving sprite
> Was none the wiser for the words he had eaten!

The Old English riddler compares gnats to a company of men:

> There is a troop of tiny folk travelling swift,
> Brought by the breeze o'er the brink of the hill,
> Buzzing black-coated bold little people,—
> Noisy musicians; well-known is their song.
> They scour the thickets, but sometimes invade
> The rooms of the town. Now tell me their names.[178]

The Old English riddler's description of mead ingeniously personifies it as a man capable of over-

---

[176] Tupper, *Exeter Book*, no. 48. The translation is by J. D. Spaeth; see his *Old English Poetry* (Princeton, 1927), p. 151.

[177] See p. 58 above.

[178] Tupper, *Exeter Book*, no. 58. The translation is by Spaeth; see p. 152.

throwing his adversary. Robert Burns conceived John Barleycorn as a man able to trip another by the heels. The Old English riddler writes:

> I'm prized by men, in the meadows I'm found,
> Gathered on the hill-sides, and hunted in groves;
> From dale and from down, by day I am brought.
> Airy wings carry me, cunningly store me,
> Hoarding me safe. Yet soon men take me;
> Drained into vats, I'm dangerous grown.
> I tie up my victim, and trip him, and throw him;
> Often I floor a foolish old churl.
> Who wrestles with me, and rashly would measure
> His strength against mine, will straightaway find himself
> Flung to the ground, flat on his back,
> Unless he leave his folly in time,
> Put from his senses and power of speech,
> Robbed of his might, bereft of his mind,
> Of his hands and feet. Now find me my name,
> Who can bind and enslave men so upon earth,
> And bring fools low in broad daylight.[179]

Some themes are borrowed from native folk song and saga; frequently, inanimate objects become endowed with life and personality; the powers of nature become objects of worship such as they were in olden times; some riddles describe the scenery of the country, the fen, the river, and the sea, the horror of the untrodden forest, sun and moon engaged in perpetual pursuit of each other, the nightingale and the swan, the plow guided by the "gray-haired enemy of the

---

[179] Tupper, *Exeter Book*, no. 28. The translation is by Spaeth; see p. 153.

wood," the bull breaking up the clods left unturned by the plow, the falcon.... Scenes, events, characters familiar in the England of that day, constantly appear in these riddles, and give them, despite what they owe to Symphosius, Aldhelm, and others, a distinctly English flavor.[180]

Sir Thomas Wyatt's description of a gun shows that the art of literary riddling was known in the English Renaissance. The text is as follows:

> Vulcan begat me: Minerva me taught:
> Nature, my mother; Craft nourisht me year by year:
> Three bodies are my foode: my strength is naught.
> Anger, wrath, waste, and noise are my children dear.
> Guess, my friend, what I am: and how I am wraught:
> Monster of sea, or of land, or of elsewhere.
> Know me, and use me: and I may thee defend:
> And if I be thine enemy, I may thy life end.[181]

The medieval German literary riddles are usually long comparisons of the parts of an object to something else. A typical example occurs in the *König Tirol*, a didactic poem of the thirteenth century: God shows Daniel a marvelous mill. It has a fixed stone below and a moving stone above. The mill wheel has seventy-two teeth. One of the teeth is of aloe wood. The son of the miller stops the lower stone, sets the upper stone in motion, and puts the mill under the care of his servant. The fixed stone is the old law and the moving stone the new law. The seventy-two teeth

---

[180] See *The Cambridge History of English Literature* (New York, Macmillan, 1933), Vol. I, pp. 66–67.
[181] Tottel's *Miscellany* (1557). Ed. E. Arber (London, 1870), p. 82.

are the seventy-two languages. The tooth of aloe wood symbolizes the Virgin Mary. The son of the miller is Jesus Christ, who stops the operation of the old law and sets in operation the new law and puts the church (the mill) under the care of his servant (the priest).[182]

Such an allegory puzzles us with its complexity. Much more interesting is Hans Folz's

> It was proclaimed in a symbol
> And later became a creature,
> And for especial strength and virtue
> It was cut in its youth.
> Its clothes grew along with it,
> Its course here on earth was barefoot,
> It was both betrayed and sold
> And baptized only when grown up,
> It shed its blood for our sakes
> So that we might put ill-humour at peace.
> It died for man's sake.
> It has also brought it to pass for us
> That we partake of it gladly with wine.[183]

---

[182] For discussion of the symbolism see Alois Thomas, *Die Darstellung Christi in der Kelter* ("Forschungen zur Volkskunde," XX, XXI, Düsseldorf, 1936), esp. pp. 163–169. For the bibliography of *König Tirol* see Gustav Ehrismann, *Geschichte der deutschen Literatur bis zum Ausgang des Mittelalters*, Schlussband (Munich, 1935), pp. 314–316; L. Wolff, "Mühlenlied," in *Verfasserlexicon des deutschen Mittelalters*, III (Berlin, 1938), cols. 441–443. Barthel Regenbogen, one of the Twelve Masters of the Meistersinger, and others, versified the theme; see Philipp Wackernagel, *Das deutsche Kirchenlied*, Vol. II (Leipzig, 1867), p. 255, no. 419, and pp. 865–869, nos. 1067–1069. For a more popular version see Edward Schröder, "Die Ebstorfer Liederhandschrift," *Jahrbuch des Vereins für niederdeutsche Sprachforschung*, XV (1890), 6–7.

[183] (Mone's) *Anzeiger für Kunde der teutschen Vorzeit*, VIII (1839), cols. 317–318, no. 97 = F. Zarncke, "Ein Spruch und ein Räthsel von Hans Folz," *Zeitschrift für deutsches Altertum*, VIII (1851). For parallels see

The "proclaiming in a symbol" is probably the cackling of the hen, and the story that Christ's seamless robe grew as our Savior's body grew explains the reference to the clothes. The riddler's suggestion of the life of Christ might seem blasphemous today, but the medieval listener was not shocked.

A debate between the mythical Klingsor, whose name and fame survive in Wagner's *Parsifal*, and Wolfram von Eschenbach is narrated in the thirteenth-century *Wartburgkrieg*. It consists of allegorical riddles and their interpretations. As an example, I choose one that has been called a masterpiece of Christian symbolism: "The lord Solomon, a powerful king, had a praiseworthy high throne made of gold and ivory with six steps on each side. Twelve young lions lay on the steps. Now note, master, what this splendor means! Two large lions stood apart, one on each side. The throne was embraced by two beautiful arms. King Solomon sat therein powerful and mighty" (Rompelman, p. 207). As Wolfram explains, this is not really Solomon's throne described in I Kings, 10: 18–20. The king is God, the throne is Mary, the

Reinhold Köhler, *Weimarisches Jahrbuch*, V (1856), 348, no. 24, reprinted in his *Kleinere Schriften*, III (Berlin, 1900), 525–528, no. 24 (with many parallels); W. L. de Vreese, *Tijdschrift voor nederlandsche taal- en letterkunde*, XX (1901), 262–263, no. 13; F. Rosenberg, *Ueber eine Sammlung deutscher Volks- und Gesellschaftslieder in hebräischen Lettern* (Berlin diss.: Brunswick, 1888), p. 34 (reprinted from *Zeitschrift für die Geschichte der Juden in Deutschland*, II [1888]). For survival of the theme in modern oral tradition see Arno Schmidt, *Hundert alte und neue Volksrätsel* (Danzig, 1924), no. 3; E. L. Rochholz, *Alemannisches Kinderlied und Kinderspiel* (Leipzig, 1857), p. 228, no 21; and Amast Joos, *Raadsels van het vlaamsche volk* (Brussels, n.d.), nos. 352, 353.

gold signifies power, the ivory the chastity of Mary, and the twelve steps the Apostles. The right-hand lion is Gabriel and the left-hand one John the Evangelist. The two arms are Simeon (Luke, 2: 28) and Joseph, who embraced Christ. King Solomon is Christ.

A last suggestion of this sort goes back to "Torcular calcavi solus" of Isaiah,[184] from which a medieval riddler[185] derived a comparison of the suffering of Christ and the making of wine, and in modern times Julia Ward Howe took the theme of

My eyes have seen the glory of the coming of the Lord;
He is trampling out the vintage where the grapes of wrath
 are stored.

The Biblical riddles in the *Christlicher Zeitvertreiber oder geistliches Rätselbuch* (1593–1597) by Michael Sachs are merely didactic, catechetical questions without a trace of literary polish.[186] Typical are such queries as "How many chapters are there in these twenty-seven books of the New Testament?—Two hundred and sixty"; "Who were the most unequal fighters?—Goliath and David"; "Who has the highest

---

[184] 63:3.

[185] See Wilhelm Wackernagel, "Sechzig Räthsel und Fragen," *Zeitschrift für deutsches Altertum*, III (1843), 27, no. 1; A. F. Butsch (ed.), *Strassburger Räthselbuch* (Strassburg, 1876), p. 1, no. 1. For the theme see also the picture in Wilhelm Pessler, *Handbuch der deutschen Volkskunde* (Potsdam, 1935), I, Pl. VII (opp. p. 217); Alois Thomas, *Die Darstellung Christi in der Kelter* ("Forschungen zur Volkskunde," XX, XXI, Düsseldorf, 1936); Hans Vollmer, "Bibel und Gewerbe in alter Zeit. Kelter und Mühle zur Veranschaulichung kirchlicher Heilsvorstellungen," *7. Bericht des Deutschen Bibelarchivs in Hamburg* (Hamburg, 1937).

[186] I am indebted to Professor John G. Kunstmann, of the University of Chicago, for the information about this rare book.

praise among all the children of men?—John the Baptist."

The history of the literary riddle in Spain has not previously been surveyed.[187] The few riddles in the medieval *Libro de Apolonio* can be passed over with brief mention, inasmuch as the work is a translation and not an original Spanish work. The riddles in it are of popular origin, for the most part, but translators and adapters, as for example Heinrich von Neustadt, have not hesitated to introduce new materials of their own invention. There are some riddles exhibiting literary rather than popular characteristics in the fifteenth-century *Cancionero* of Juan Alfonso de Baena, but the number is so small that we cannot speak of an active practice of literary riddling at this time.[188] Many of them are *preguntas* or questions on some vague subject requiring an answer that is often given by another poet in exactly the same rhyme scheme. An excellent example is the following *desir*, written by Francisco Imperial, "commo á manera de pregunta é de adevinança sobre el amor":

> Yo me sso uno que bivo
> con todo omme ó muger,
> é non me veen, magüer
> á muchos é á muchas privo
> la vista; é soy esquivo
> é plasentero á la veses,

---

[187] I follow here the collectanea of Demófilo (Antonio Machado y Álvarez) in his *Adivinanzas* (Seville, 1880), pp. 482–492. Several small collections are here passed over without mention.

[188] See Demófilo, p. 484.

é en poder de rrafezes
á grandes echo en cativo.

Yo mesmo ardo en fuego
é de sí çenisa quando,
é despues muy quedo á quedo
todo en uno me llego,
é qual era torrno luego;
é de madre non nasçí,
nin tal qual so nunca vý
demudado torrno viego.

Alfonso Álvares de Villasandino answered Imperial's *desir* as follows:

Yo non leo bien, nin escrivo;
pero ¿que oý leer?
Angel fueste Lusifer;
mas tornaste algarivo.
Por non ser caritativo,
yases fondo de las feses,
do el mundo, por sus jaeses,
traes emaginativo.

Tu ardes, é non por juego,
en lugar amargo é asedo,
donde non sse rresa el credo;
despues tornas todo entrego,
oras murueco é borrego
te torrnas por mal de tý.
Non respondo mas aquí,
que so ynorante lego.[189]

---

[189] *El Cancionero* de Juan Alfonso de Baena (Leipzig: Brockhaus, 1880), Vol. I, pp. 232–233.

The *Respuestas à las cuatrocientas preguntas del Almirante D. Fadrique*. Por Luis Escobar (d. 1552),[190] which was published at Valladolid in 1545, is perhaps the earliest important collection of literary riddles in Spain. It does not appear to have been reprinted in recent times. The *Cancionero* de Sebastián de Horozco (not printed till 1874), a Toledan author,[191] contains a number of interesting riddles. A very familiar one is the *enigma del año*. In Horozco's *Cancionero* (p. 247) it is worded as follows:

> Doze hijos quasi iguales
> vi á un padre que tenía
> y cada qual destos tales,
> legítimas, naturales
> sus treynta hijas habia.
> La mitad de aquestas era
> de clara y blanca color,
> y por contraria manera
> la otra mitad saliera
> de turbio y triste negror.
>
> Y vi qu'estas hijas tales
> de tal suerte procedian
> que todas eran mortales,
> tambien eran inmortales
> segun que se sucedian.
> Y trataban comunmente
> con los hombres como amigas,
> pero despues de repente
> en el tpo. mas urgente
> huyan como enemigas.

---

[190] See Demófilo, p. 483.   [191] See Demófilo, p. 487.

In a footnote at the bottom of the page, we are told: "Esta enigma escribió Cleobulo, como trae Diogenes Laercio; y lo refiere el comendador y comentador de Las *Trecientas* de Juan de Mena, en la primera copla de la cuarta orden de Phebo." It is a well-known fact, of course, that Laertius did ascribe this riddle to Cleobulus. Hicks translates it thus:

One sire there is, he has twelve sons, and each of these has twice thirty daughters different in feature: some of the daughters are white, the others again are black; they are immortal, and yet they all die.[192]

Sir Thomas Wyatt versified this as follows:

> One is my sire: my soons, twise six they bee:
> Of daughters each of them begets, you see,
> Twise ten: whereof one sort be fayr of face,
> The oother doth unseemly black disgrace.
> Nor this hall rout is thrall vnto deathdaye,
> Nor worn with wastfull time, but liue alwaye:
> And the same alwaies (straunge case) do dye.
> The fire, the daughters, and the soons distry.
> In case you can so hard a knot vnknit:
> You shall I count an Edipus in wit.[193]

Several riddles in Horozco's *Cancionero*, such as *la hormiga* (ant), *relox* (watch), *padilla* (frying pan), *hermafrodito* (from Politian), are given in the usual form of *preguntas y respuestas*, quite similar to those

---

[192] Diogenes Laertius, *Lives of Eminent Philosophers*, trans. R. D. Hicks (Loeb Classical Library, New York, Putnam, 1925), I, 93.

[193] Tottel's *Miscellany* (London, 1557). Ed. E. Arber (London, 1870), p. 102. For other versions of the year see De Filippis, pp. 14, 59–60, 77.

of Baena. *La padilla*, which is reproduced here with its answer, is typical of most of them:

> Dezidme, qual es la cosa milagrosa
> que de bocas tres alcanza,
> y es en sí tan tenebrosa
> y espantosa
> que por todas fuego lanza?
> Una boca desta alhaja come paja,
> nunca bebe con ninguna;
> otra tiene tal ventaja;
> aunque trabaja,
> que con pan se desayuna.

> Aunque parece ser cosa espantosa,
> y que su ser no se alcança,
> quedará sin ser dudosa
> ni escabrosa,
> y sin ninguna dudança.
> Tres bocas tiene esta alhaja,
> que con paja
> se calienta por la una,
> y es padilla do se quaxa
> lo que ataja
> á toda hambre importuna.[194]

El trigo (wheat), on page 121, is longer than several others, but should be quoted because it has much in common with Halevi's version:

> ¿Quién es aquel sin el qual
> ninguno vive contento?
> este hecho terrenal
> para el linaje humanal

---

[194] *Cancionero* (ed. 1874), pp. 120–121.

dirije su nacimiento;
mas despues es despojado
de todas sus vestiduras
arrastrado y maltratado,
hasta morir sepultado
por bien de las criaturas.

Y aqueste muerto, quedando
los hijos, que dél suceden,
se van sin padre criando,
creciendo y multiplicando
hasta ya que mas no pueden.
Pero siendo ya crecidos,
en presencia de su madre
son a cuchillo metidos,
y muchos dellos traidos
á lo mesmo que su padre.

Y otros muchos dellos son
por fuerça despedaçados
sin ninguna compasion,
dó sin mucha dilacion
quedan en polvo tornados.
Con el húmido elemento
juntados aquestos tales,
despues con fuego y tormento
son hechos mantenimiento
de infinitos animales.

Although some of the riddles in this collection are too obscene to reprint, Demófilo considers the work worthy of further study.

A little later, Alexandre Sylvain (or: Alexander van den Bussche) printed his *Qvarentas Aenigmas en lengua espannola*.[195] This booklet contains nine original riddles of his own and thirty-one "de varios avthores." He does not name his sources, but Straparola or the collections on which Straparola drew are among them.[196] Those for which I have not found parallels in Straparola are presumably borrowed from Italian collections.

The most important Spanish author to compose riddles was Cervantes, who included several in his *Galatea*, written in 1585.[197] In addition to his riddle defining a riddle, already quoted,[198] he treated enigmatically wine (*vino*), coal (*carbon*), letter and writing paper (*carta y pliego de cartas*), jealousy (*celosia*), man in chains (*hombre con grillos*), shears to snuff a candle (*tigeras de despauilar*), and the following, for which no solution is given:

> Tres hijos que de una madre
> nascieron con ser perfecto,
> y de un hermano era nieto
> el uno, y el otro padre;

[195] Paris, 1581. In the copy accessible to me the Spanish riddles have their own title page and are bound in front of *Cinquante Aenigmes Françoises*, d'Alexandre Sylvain . . . Ensemble quelques Aenigmes Espagnolles dudict Autheur, & d'autres (Paris, 1582). Both books are in the British Museum; see the entry in the catalogue under Alexander van den Bussche. For other citations see De Backer, I, 412; Brunet, *Manuel*, I, 1420, and *Supplement*, I, 188. Palau y Dulcet, VI, 599, could not cite a copy.

[196] For a detailed discussion of this work see De Filippis, pp. 51 ff.

[197] Demófilo, p. 486.

[198] See pp. 5–6 above.

y estos tres tan sin clemencia
a su madre ma[e] tratavan,
que mil puñadas la davan,
mostrando en ello su sciencia.[199]

In an excellent discussion of Portuguese popular traditions, Theofilo Braga cites several instances of the literary use of popular riddles at the time of the Renaissance.[200] In Gil Vicente's *Auto pastoril caste-lhano*, which was written in 1502, a company engage in riddling. One asks, "What animal runs and runs and is not seen?" Another replies, "Mortal sin," and a dispute follows in which a third speaker defends the folk answer, "the wind." The grammar of João de Barros, published in 1538, contains the generally known riddle comparing smoke to a son who goes about before his father, the fire, is born. Such examples show that both authors and scholars knew folk riddles similar to those circulating today. Braga directs attention to two collections of literary riddles: Francisco Lopes, *Passatempo honesto de enigmas e adivinhações* (1603), and Soror María de Céo, *Enganos de bosque, desenganos de rio* (1741). The later work falls outside the limit I have set myself, and will receive no consideration. I shall, therefore, repeat here only a few quotations from the very rare *Passatempo*.

---

[199] *Galatea*, Book VI, pp. 255–263. See also Rudolph Schevill, *Some Forms of the Riddle Question and the Exercise of the Wits in Popular Fiction and Formal Literature* (Univ. Calif. Publ. Mod. Philol. [1911]), pp. 219 ff.

[200] *O povo portuguez* (Lisbon, 1886), II, 374–383. J. Leite da Vasconcellos probably gives some additional information in an article on riddles in *Lusa*, III, 137 ff.; but this rare journal, which was published at Viana do Castelo from 1917 to 1924, has been inaccessible to me.

Braga notes with interest the occurrence of the same themes and often the same rhymes in the *Passatempo* and in modern folklore versions. No attempt will be made here to determine whether the versifier of the *Passatempo* kept the rhymes that he found in a folk version or whether the modern folk version has descended to us from the *Passatempo*. Suffice it to note the similarity of the Renaissance riddle for pins:

> Somos quinhentos soldados
> De nossas armas compostos,
> Todos cobertos e armados,
> Em fileiras ordenados,
> E n'um campo branco postos.
>   Não já para pelejar
> Porque não somos temidos,
> Antes de damas queridos,
> Que nos põem n'um alto logar
> Onde andamos escondidos,

and the modern folk version from Alemtejo:

> Quatrocentos soldados
> Formados n'um campo branco,
> Nós não somos destemidos,
> Somos das damas quiridos,
> Que nos trazem em salvos logares
> D'onde andamos escondidos.

Braga quotes riddles for day and night; the months, days of the week, and year; a ball of thread; and a leek. The first of these repeats the same conception of a cosmological theme that we have met before, but

with some minor variations of its own. In conjunction
with the previous quotation, it will supply an adequate idea of the *Passatempo:*

> O dia e a noite
>
> Um homem e uma mulher
> Grandes inimigos são,
> Que nunca se podem vêr,
> E ambos sem descansar vão
> Um apoz outro correr.
>   Elle é formoso e bello
> Como a folha de uma rosa;
> Ella nunca póde vêl-o
> E e tal que lhe põem o sello
> Da mais feia e mais perigosa.

The first French collection of literary riddles is apparently Charles Fontaine's *Odes, énigmes et épigrammes*, which was printed at Lyons in 1557. According
to Brunet,[201] Fontaine versified twenty-eight riddles
from the collection of Symphosius. He therefore rep-
resents a learned and literary tradition quite different
from such earlier collections of folk materials as the
Adeuineaux amoureux, which was compiled in the last
quarter of the fifteenth century.[202] The *Questions
énigmatiques, récréatives et propres pour deviner et y
passer les temps aux veillées des longues nuicts*[203] and

---

[201] *Manuel*, 5th ed., Vol. II, col. 1327, no. 3.
[202] *Gesamtkatalog der Wiegendrucke*, I (Leipzig, 1925), nos. 222 and 223.
There was a reprint at Paris in 1831.
[203] Lyons, 1568 and 1583. Cited from Brunet, *Manuel*, IV, col. 1015, and
Alfred Canel, *Recherches sur les jeux d'esprit* (Evreux, 1867), I, 379–380.

the *Questions et démandes récréatives pour resjouir les esprits mélancoliques*[204] of the second half of the sixteenth century are also potpourris of folk stuff and need only be mentioned here as examples of the current interest in riddles, conundrums, and witty questions. In 1582, a year after the appearance of his Spanish collection, Alexandre Sylvain (Alexander van den Bussche) published *Cinquante Aenigmes*. Although he says in his preface that he composed them, several were clearly suggested by Italian originals.[205]

In the seventeenth century, riddling was much favored in French literary circles,[206] but this activity belongs to a time much later than the limits of this survey.

We have now reached the end of this brief account of literary riddling. By 1600, it had attained recognition as a genre in anthologies given over exclusively to riddles and in treatises reviewing the history and technique of the art. In Italy, literary riddling continued to flourish. In France, it enjoyed greater esteem during the seventeenth and eighteenth centuries than it had won before. In contemporary German baroque literature, there were some reflections of this Italian and French enthusiasm, but these faded in the eighteenth century, when pietism and rationalism gained the upper hand. In England, the literary riddle has never found wide acceptance and

---

[204] Paris, 1573, 1576, 1583. Cited from Brunet, *Manuel*, IV, col. 1015, and from Cancl.

[205] For discussion see De Filippis, pp. 54 ff.

[206] For titles see Archer Taylor, *Bibliography of Riddles*, pp. 58–61.

use, although Dean Swift and others tried their hands at writing it. In Germany, and especially in Austria, in the second half of the nineteenth century, German writers turned once more to literary riddles. The Italian enthusiasm for the enigmatic art is perhaps the climax of literary interest in riddling; it took form in several journals and handbooks as well as many individual collections. A study of these developments may follow on another occasion.

BIBLIOGRAPHY

Abrahams, Israel. Jewish Life in the Middle Ages. New York, Macmillan, 1896, 1907, etc.

Les Adeuineaux amoureux. Bruges, Colard Mansion, *ca.* 1478. Reprinted in the series "Joyeusetés facéties," VI. Paris, Techener, 1831.

Aenigmata et griphi veterum ac recentium. Douai, Carolus Boscardus, 1604.

Allgemeine deutsche Biographie. Leipzig, Duncker und Humblot, 1875–1912.

Aluny, Nehemya. "Ten [of] Dunash ben Labrat's Riddles," Jewish Quarterly Review, XXXVI (1945–1946), 141–146.

Anthologia graeca. Ed. F. Jacobs. Leipzig, Dyck, 1794–1804.

Anzeiger für Kunde der teutschen Vorzeit. [Title varies.] 1832–1839. *See* Berne Riddles.

Atharvaveda. *See* Haug.

Athenaeus Naucratica. Deipnosophistarum libri XV.

Backer, Augustin and Alois de, and Carol Sommervogel, Bibliothèque de la Compagnie de Jésus. Nouv. éd. Brussels, O. Schepens, 1890–1909.

Baena, Juan Alfonso de. El Cancionero. Publicado por Francisco Michel. Leipzig, Brockhaus, 1880.

Barbara, Franciscus a S. Oedipodiana seu Sphingis Aenigmata. Milan, Federicus Blancus, 1720. Oppau, Johannes W. Schindler, 1732.

Basset, René. [Review of A. Giacobetti, Recueil d'énigmes arabes, Algiers, 1916], Revue des traditions populaires, XXXII (1916–1917), 186–190.

Beiträge zur Assyriologie. *See* Jaeger.

Bellamy, William. A Century of Charades. Boston, Houghton, Mifflin & Co., 1896.

Berne Riddles. F. J. Mone, Anzeiger für Kunde der teutschen Vorzeit, VIII (1839), 219–229; H. Hagen, Antike und mittelalterliche Rätselpoesie (Biel, 1869), pp. 25–27 and (Bern, 1877) pp. 25–27; P. Brandt, Tirocin. philol. sod. reg. sem. (Bonn, 1883), pp. 101–133 [not seen]; Wilhelm Meyer, Abhandlungen der bayerischen Akademie, philologisch-philosophische Klasse, XVII (1886), 417–430; Riese, Anthologia latina (Leipzig, 1870), I, 296–304, and II, p. xlvi; 2d ed. (Leipzig, 1894), I, 350–370.

Bielenstein, A. Tausend lettische Rätsel. Mitau, E. Sieslack, 1881.

Binder, Wilhelm. Flores aenigmatum latinorum. Stuttgart, Metzler, 1857.

Boissonade, J. F. Anecdota graeca e codicibus regiis. Paris, Regius typographicus, 1829–1833.

Boniface. *See* Dümmler.

Booke of Merrie Riddles. London, Robert Bird, 1631. Reprinted in Brandl, pp. 53–63.

Braga, Theofilo. O povo portuguez. Lisbon, Livraria Ferreira, 1885.

Brandl, Alois. "Shakespeares 'Book of Merry Riddles' und die andern Rätselbücher seiner Zeit," Jahrbuch der Deutschen Shakespeare-Gesellschaft, XLII (1906), 1–64. Cited as Brandl.

Brockelmann, Carl. Geschichte der arabischen Literatur. Weimar, Felber, 1898–1902.

Brunet, Jacques-Charles. Manuel du libraire. 5th ed. Paris, Firmin Didot frères, 1860–1865.

Buchler, Johannes. Gnomologia seu sententiarum memorabilium, cum primis Germanicae Gallicaeque linguae, brevis et aperta, Latino carmine, inspersis rhythmis festivissimis, facta descriptio. Cologne, 1602; Cologne, Bernardus Gualtherus, 1606; Mainz, Johannes Volmar, 1614; Cologne, Hartger Woringen, 1639.

Butsch, A. F. *See* Strassburger Räthselbuch.

Camerarius, Joachim, the Elder. Elementa Rhetoricae. Basel, J. Oporinus, 1545. *Ibid.*, 1551. Leipzig, Officina Vogeliana, 1564.

Canel, Alfred. Recherches sur les jeux d'esprit. Évreux, A. Hérrissey, 1867.

Catone l'Uticense Lucchese. Enimmi. Parma, F. Carpignani, 1760.

———. Enimmi. Con aggiunta di altri autori. Genoa, Franchelli, 1761.

Céo, Soror Maria de. Engaños de bosque, desengaños de rio. 1741. Cited from Braga.

Cervantes Saavedra, Miguel de. La Galatea, ed. Rudolph Schevill and A. Bonilla y San Martín. Madrid, B. Rodríguez, 1914.

Chambers, Robert. Popular Rhymes of Scotland. London, W. and R. Chambers, 1870.

Chauvin, Victor. Bibliographie des ouvrages arabes. Liége, H. Vaillant-Carmanne, 1892–1922.

Chenery, Thomas (transl.). *See* Al-Harîrî.

Chiariti, S. Enimmi da indovinare. Venice, Graziosi, 1784.

Croce, G. C. Notte sollazzevole di cento enigmi da indovinare. Con VII sonetti del medesimo genere. Venice, A. de' Vecchi, 1599.

Crosnier, Abbé Aug.-Jos. Sacramentarium ad usum Aecclesiae Nivernensis. Nevers, 1873.

Demófilo. *See* Máchado y Álvarez, Antonio.

Destunis, G. S. "Ocherki grecheskoi zagadki s drevnikh
vremen do novykh," Zhurnal ministerstva narodnago
prosvescheniia, CCLXX (1890), 66–98, 262–290.

Deutsche morgenländische Gesellschaft. *See* Führer; Rosen;
Roth.

Deutsche Shakespeare-Gesellschaft. *See* Brandl.

Dictionnaire d'archéologie chrétienne et de liturgie. Paris,
Letouzy et Ané, 1903 et seqq.

Dilthey, Karl. Symbolae criticae ad Anthologiam graecam
ex libris manuscriptis petitae. *In*: Index lectionum für
das Sommersemester, 1891. Göttingen, 1891.

Dümmler, Ernest. Poetae latini aevi Carolini. *In* Monumenta Germaniae historica, Poetarum latinorum medii
aevi, I (Berlin, 1881), 1–15, "Bonifatii carmina."

Ebert, Adolf. "Ueber der Räthselpoesie der Angelsachsen,
insbesondere die Aenigmata des Tatwine und Eusebius,"
Berichte über die Verhandlungen d. k. sächsischen Gesellschaft d. Wissenschaften, phil.-hist. Classe, XXIX
(1877), 20–56.

Ehrismann, Gustav. Geschichte der deutschen Literatur
bis zum Ausgang des Mittelalters. Schlussband. Munich,
C. H. Beck'sche Verlagsbuchhandlung, 1935.

Escobar, Fr. Luis. Respuestas a las cuatrocientas preguntas
del Almirante D. Fadrique. Valladolid, 1545. Cited from
Rodríguez Marín, I, 314, n. 1.

Eusebius. *See* Ebert.

Eustachius (Eustathius) Macrembolites. *See* Hilberg.

Fabricius, Johann Albert. Bibliotheca graeca. Ed. C. G.
Harles. Hamburg, C. E. Bohn, and (Vol. 13) Leipzig,
Cnobloch, 1790–1809.

Fabricius, Johann Albert. Bibliotheca mediae et infimae latinitatis. Florence, T. Baracchi et f., 1858–1859.

Flajšhans, Vaclav. Klaret a jeho družina. Prague, 1926–1928.

Fontaine, Charles. Odes, énigmes et épigrammes. Lyons, J. Citoys, 1557. Cited from Brunet.

Fosterus, Johannes. Centuria prima selectissimorum juxta, et variae jucunditatis aenigmatum. Leipzig, 1602. Not seen.

Friedreich, J. B. Geschichte des Räthsels. Dresden, Rudolf Kuntze, 1860.

Führer, A. "Sanskrit-Räthsel," Zeitschrift der Deutschen morgenländischen Gesellschaft, XXXIX (1885), 99–100.

Gibb, E. J. W. A History of Ottoman Literature. London, Luzac & Co., 1901–1907.

Gifford, Humphrey. Posie of Gillowflowers. London, 1580. Reprinted in Brandl, "Noch eine Rätselsammlung der Shakespeare-Zeit," Jahrbuch der Deutschen Shakespeare-Gesellschaft, XLV (1909), 139–145.

Giraldi, Lilio Gregorio. Aenigmatum ex antiquis scriptoribus collectorum libellus singularis. Basel, J. Oporinus, 1551. Reprinted in his Opera (Basel, T. Guarinus, 1580) and in Nicolaus Reusner, Aenigmatographia (Frankfurt a. M., 1599; 2d ed., *ibid.*, 1602). The two earliest editions not seen.

Goedeke, Karl. Grundriss zur Geschichte der deutschen Dichtung. 2d ed., Dresden, L. Ehlermann, 1884–.

Hall, Bishop Joseph. Mundus alter et idem. Frankfurt a. M., n.d. [actually: London, H. Lownes, 1605]. Hanau, 1607. Cited from Dictionary of National Biography; not in Pollard and Redgrave, Short-Title Catalogue. Utrecht, 1643.

Hammer-Purgstall, Joseph. Geschichte der osmanischen Dichtkunst. Pest, Hartleben, 1837–1838.

———. Geschichte der schönen Redekünste Persiens. Vienna, Heubner und Volke, 1818.

Al-Harîrî. The Assemblies. Translated by Thomas Chenery and F. Steingass. "Oriental Translation Fund," New Series, 3. London, Luzac & Co., 1867–1898.

Haug, [Martin]. "Vedische Räthselfragen und Räthsel-sprüche," Sitzungsberichte d. k. Akad. d. Wissenschaften, philosophisch-philologische Classe (Munich), II, No. 3 (1875).

Healey, John. Discovery of a New World, or a Description of the South Indies, hitherto unknown, by an English Mercury. London [G. Eld], for E. Blomit and W. Barrett [1609?].

Helmbold, Ludovicus. Aenigmatum centuria. N.p., n.d. A copy in the library of Archer Taylor.

Hilberg, Isidor (ed.). [Review of M. Treu, Eustathii Macrembolitae quae ferunter aenigmata], Byzantinische Zeitschrift, III (1894), 172–175.

Horozco, Sebastián de. Cancionero. Seville, Tarasco, 1874.

Hutton, James. The Greek Anthology in Italy to the Year 1800. "Cornell Studies in English," XXIII. Ithaca, Cornell University Press, 1931.

———. The Greek Anthology in France and in the Latin Writers of the Netherlands to the Year 1800. "Cornell University Studies in English," XXVIII. Cornell University Press, 1946.

Jacobs, Joseph. Jewish Ideals. London, D. Nutt, 1896.

Jaeger, M. "Assyrische Räthsel und Sprichwörter," Beiträge zur Assyriologie, II (1894), 274–305.

Joos, Amaat. Raadsels van het vlaamsche volk. Brussels, Standaard-Boekhandel, n.d. (*ca.* 1926).

Jüdisches Lexikon. Berlin, Jüdischer Verlag (*ca.* 1930).

Junius, Hadrian. Emblematum et aenigmatum libellus. Antwerp, Plantin, 1565. *Ibid.*, 1585.

Kircher, Athanasius. Oedipus Aegyptiacus. Rome, V. Mascardus, 1653.

Köhler, Reinhold. "Zwei-und-vierzig alte Rätsel und Fragen," Weimarisches Jahrbuch, V (1856), 329–356. Reprinted (with additions) in Kleinere Schriften, III (Berlin, 1900), 499–538.

Krumbacher, Karl. Geschichte der byzantinischen Literatur. 2d ed.; Munich, C. H. Beck, 1897.

Licetus (Liceti), Fortunius. Allegoria peripatetica de generatione, amicitia et privatione in Aristotelicum aenigma: Elia Lelia Crispis. Venice, 1629. Padua, G. Crivellarius, 1630. Not seen.

Lipenius, Martin. Bibliotheca realis. Frankfurt a. M., Joannes Friderici, 1679–1685. A division of this work has the subtitle: Bibliotheca philosophica.

Listy filologické. *See* Ryba.

Lopes, Francisco. Passatempo honesto de enigmas e adivinhações. Cited from Braga.

Lorichius, Johannes. Aenigmatum libri tres. Frankfurt a. M., C. Egenolph, 1545.

Lorsch Riddles. E. L. Dümmler, Zeitschrift für deutsches Altertum, XXII (1878), 258–263; *idem*, Poetae latini aevi Carolini, in Monumenta Germaniae historica, Berlin, 1881, I, 20–23.

Machado y Álvarez, Antonio (pseud. Demófilo). Colección de enigmas y adivinanzas. Seville, R. Baldaraque, 1880.

Majânî l'Adab. Beirut, 1885–1896.

Malatesti, A. La Sfinge e la Tina. Pref. di E. Allodoli. Lanciano, Carabba, 1913.

Malvasia, Y. C. C. Aelia Laelia Crispis non nata resurgens in expositione legali. Bologna, D. Barberius, 1683.

Manitius, Max. Geschichte der lateinischen Dichtung im Mittelalter. Munich, C. H. Beck'sche Verlagsbuchhandlung, 1911 et seqq.

Masenius, Jacobus. Speculum veritatis occultae. Cologne, 1650. 2d ed., I. A. Kinchius, 1664. Not seen.

Ménage, Gilles. Ménagiana. Paris, Florentin Delaulne, 1715.

Notes and Queries, 1849 et seqq.

Nyare bidrag till kännedom om de svenska landsmålen. *See* Sandén.

Ohl, R. T. The Enigmas of Symphosius. Diss. Univ. of Pennsylvania. Philadelphia, 1928.

Ohlert, Konrad. Rätsel und Rätselspiele der alten Griechen. Berlin, Mayer and Müller, 1886. 2d ed., 1912.

Palau y Dulcet, Antonio. Manual del librero hispano-americano. Barcelona, Librería anticuaria, 1923–1927.

Pessler, Wilhelm. Handbuch der deutschen Volkskunde. Potsdam, Akademische Verlagsgesellschaft Athenaion, 1935 et seqq.

Pettengill, R. W. "Zu den Rätseln des Heinrich von Neustadt," Journal of English and Germanic Philology, XII (1913), 248–251.

Pincier, Johannes. Aenigmatum libri tres. Herborn, Christophorus Corvinus, 1605. The Hague, A. Vlacq, 1665.

Pitman, John H. The Riddles of Aldhelm. "Yale Studies in English," LXVII. New Haven, Yale University Press, 1925.

Pitrè, Giuseppe. Indovinelli, dubbi, scioglilingua del popolo siciliano. Turin and Palermo, Clausen, 1897.

Pontanus (Spanmüller), Jacobus. Dialogus qui inscributur enigma. Reprinted in Nicolaus Reusner, Aenigmatographia (Frankfurt a. M., 1602).

Questions énigmatiques, récréatives et propres pour deviner et y passer le temps aux veillées des longues nuicts. Lyons, B. Rigaut, 1568. Cited from Brunet, Manuel, 5th ed., IV, col. 1015.

Questions et démandes récréatives pour resjouir les esprits mélancoliques. Paris, Ant. Houic, 1573. Paris, pour Jean de l'Astre, 1576. Cited from Brunet, Manuel, 5th ed., IV, col. 1015.

Reusner, Nicolaus. Aenigmata. Frankfurt a. M., Collegium Musarum Palthenianum, 1601.

———. Aenigmatographia. Frankfurt a. M., Georg Draud and Philipp Angelus, 1599. Frankfurt a. M., Collegium Musarum Palthenianum, 1602.

The Riddles of Heraclitus and Democritus. London, An. Hatfield for John Norton, 1598. In Brandl, pp. 31–51.

Rochholz, E. L. Alemannisches Kinderlied und Kinderspiel. Leipzig, J. J. Weber, 1857.

Rodríguez Marín, F. Cantos populares españoles. Seville, F. Álvarez y Ca., 1882–1883.

Rolland, Eugène. Devinettes ou énigmes populaires de la France. Paris, F. Vieweg, 1877.

Rompelman, T. A. Der Wartburgkrieg kritisch herausgegeben. Amsterdam, H. J. Paris, 1939.

Rosen, Gustav. "Proben neuerer gelehrter Dichtkunst der Araber," Zeitschrift der Deutschen morgenländischen Gesellschaft, XIII (1859), 249–255; XIV (1860), 692–705; XX (1866), 589–595; XXII (1868), 541–544.

Rosenberg, F. Ueber eine Sammlung deutscher Volks- und Gesellschaftslieder in hebräischen Lettern. Diss. Univ. of Berlin. Brunswick, 1888.

Roth, R. "Zwei Sprüche über Leib und Seele," Zeitschrift der Deutschen morgenländischen Gesellschaft, XLVI (1892), 759–760.

Rudolph, Richard C. "Notes on the Riddle in China," California Folklore Quarterly, I (1942), 65–82.

Ryba, Bohumil. "Klaretovo autorství enigmatiku," Listy filologické, LXIV (1937), 266–267.

Sachs, Michael. Der christliche Zeitvertreiber oder geistliches Rätzelbuch, Der erste Theil. Dresden, Gimel Nicol, 1593. Das ander Theil, 1597.

Sandén, P. A. "Gåtor från Fredsbargs ock församlingar in Norra Vadsbo härad," Nyare bidrag till kännedom om de svenska landsmålen, VII, 4 (1887).

Scaliger, Julius Caesar. Poemata. [Heidelberg], P. Santanderanus, 1591.

———. Poetices. [Lyons, A. Vincentius], 1561. [Heidelberg], In bibliopolio Commeliano, 1617.

Schelhorn, J. G. Amoenitates literariae. Frankfurt a. M., D. Bartholomaei et fil., 1725–1731.

Schevill, Rudolph. Some Forms of the Riddle Question and the Exercise of the Wits in Popular Fiction and Formal Literature. Univ. Calif. Publ. Mod. Philol., Vol. III, No. 3, Berkeley, 1911.

Schmidt, Arno. Hundert alte und neue Volksrätsel. "Heimatblätter des deutschen Heimatbundes," I. Danzig, A. W. Kafemann, 1924.

Schröder, Edward. "Die Ebstorfer Liederhandschrift," Jahrbuch des Vereins für niederdeutsche Sprachforschung, XV (1890), 1–32.

Scott, Walter. The Antiquary. Edinburgh, A. Constable and Co., 1816.

Sébillot, Paul. "Devinettes recueillés dans les Côtes-du-Nord et l'Ille-et-Vilaine," Bulletins et Mémoires de la Société d'émulation des Côtes-du-Nord, XXIII (Saint-Bricuc, 1885), Mémoires, pp. 93–115.

Simrock, Karl. Das deutsche Rätselbuch. 3d ed., Basel, n.d.

Spaeth, J. Duncan. Old English Poetry. Princeton University Press, 1927.

Spanmüller, Johannes. *See* Pontanus.

Steingass, F. *See* Al-Ḥarîrî.

Stigliani, T. Rime. Venice, G. B. Ciotti, 1605.

Straparola, M. Giovanfrancesco. Le Piacevoli Notti. A cura de G. Rua. Bologna, Romagnoli-Dall'Acqua, 1899–1908.

Strassburger Räthselbuch. Ed. A. F. Butsch. Strassburg, K. J. Trübner, 1876.

Suchier, Walther. L'Enfant sage (Das Gespräch des Kaisers Hadrian mit dem klugen Kinde Epitus). "Gesellschaft für romanische Literatur," XXIV. Dresden, 1910.

Sylvain, Alexandre (Alexandro Sylvano, Alexander van den Bussche). Cinquante Aenigmes françoises. Paris, Gilles Beys, 1582.

———. Quarenta Aenigmas en lengua espannola. Paris, Giles Beys, 1581.

Taylor, Archer. A Bibliography of Riddles. "FF Communications," CXXVI. Helsinki, Finnish Academy of Sciences, 1939.

———. English Riddles from Oral Tradition. In press.

Thomas, Alois. Die Darstellung Christi in der Kelter. "Forschungen zur Volkskunde," XX, XXI. Düsseldorf, Schwann, 1936.

Tijdschrift voor nederlandsche taal- en letterkunde. *See* De Vreese.

Torczyner, Harry. "The Riddle in the Bible," Hebrew Union College Annual, I (1924), 125–150.

Tottel's Miscellany (London, 1557). Reprinted in E. Arber, ed., English Reprints. London, 1870.

Treu, M. Eustathii Macrembolitae quae ferunter aenigmata. Programm, Breslau, 1893.

Tritheim, Johannes. De scriptoribus ecclesiasticis. Basel, Johannes Amerbach, 1494.

Tupper, Frederick. "The Comparative Study of Riddles," Modern Language Notes, XVIII (1903), 1–8.

———. "The Holme Riddles (MS. Harl. 1960)," Publications of the Modern Language Association, XVIII (1903), 211–272.

———. The Riddles of the Exeter Book. "The Albion Series of Anglo-Saxon and Middle English Poetry." Boston, Ginn and Co., 1910.

Turrius, Joannes. Epistola super aenigmata Aelia Laelia Crispis. Dordrecht, 1618. Not seen.

Verein für niederdeutsche Sprachforschung. Jahrbuch. *See* Schröder.

Verfasserlexikon des deutschen Mittelalters. Berlin, W. de Gruyter, 1933 et seqq.

Vollmer, Hans. "Bibel und Gewerbe in alter Zeit. Kelter und Mühle zur Veranschaulichung kirchlicher Heilsvorstellungen," 7. Bericht des Deutschen Bibelarchivs in Hamburg. Hamburg, 1937.

Vreese, W. L. de. "Middelnederlandsche geestelijke gedichten, liederen en rijmen," Tijdschrift voor nederlandsche taal- en letterkunde, XX (1901), 249–290.

Vries, Jan de. Die Märchen von den klugen Rätsellösern. "FF Communications," LXXIII. Helsinki, Finnish Academy of Sciences, 1928.

Wackernagel, Philipp. Das deutsche Kirchenlied. Leipzig, B. G. Teubner, 1864–1877.

Wackernagel, Wilhelm. "Sechzig Räthsel und Fragen," Zeitschrift für deutsches Altertum, III (1843), 25–34.

Wartburgkrieg. *See* Rompelman.

Weimarisches Jahrbuch. *See* Köhler.

Wesselski, Albert. "Die gelehrten Sklavinnen und ihre byzantinischen Vorbilder," Archiv orientální, IX (1937), 333–378.

White, Richard. Aelia Laelia Crispis Epitaphium Antiquum quod in agro Bononiensi adhuc videtur, a diversis interpretatum varie, novissime autem ... explicatum. Padua, 1568. Not seen.

Wilmanns, Wilhelm. "Disputatio regalis et nobilissimi iuvenis Pippini cum Albino scholastico," Zeitschrift für deutsches Altertum, XIV (1869), 530–555.

Winternitz, Moritz. A History of Indian Literature. [Calcutta], Univ. of Calcutta, 1927 et seqq.

Wünsche, August. Der babylonische Talmud. Leipzig, 1886–1889.

———. Die Rätselweisheit bei den alten Hebräern mit Hinblick auf andere alte Völker. Leipzig, 1883.

Zarncke, Friedrich. "Ein Spruch und ein Räthsel von Hans Folz," Zeitschrift für deutsches Altertum, VIII (1851), 537–542.

Zeitschrift für deutsches Altertum. *See* Lorsch Riddles; Wackernagel; Wilmanns; Zarncke.

INDEX OF RIDDLEMASTERS

INDEX OF SOLUTIONS